NON NOM YOUR WAY TO NOT FEELING LIKE GARBAGE

A SASS-FILLED GUIDE TO EATING BETTER, FEELING AMAZING, AND DITCHING THE BLOAT

Non Nom your way to not Feeling like Garbage

A Sass-Filled Guide to Eating Better, Feeling Amazing, and Ditching the Bloat

Irene C. Fields

© 2025 Irene Fields

All rights reserved. No part of this publication may be reproduced, distributed, or transmitted in any form or by any means, including photocopying, recording, or other electronic or mechanical methods, without the prior written permission of the publisher, except in the case of brief quotations embodied in critical reviews and certain other noncommercial uses permitted by copyright law.

First Edition

Printed in the United States of America

First Printing, March 2025.

Contents

Introduction...6

1

The Anti-Inflammatory Diet: WHAT YOU SHOULD KNOW...9

2

How to Eat the Anti-Inflammatory Way...13

3

Breakfast and First Meals...26

4

Snacks and Sides...43

5

Vegetarian and Vegan...54

6

Fish and Beef...68

7

Whole Grains and Pasta...79

8

Soups and Stews...98

9

Cortisol Detox...115

10

The Food Elimination Plan...121

4 weeks meal plan 125

Food elimination tracker 129

Recipe index 140

INTRODUCTION

Dear Reader,

Right now, as you hold this book, your body may be fighting a battle you cannot see. Perhaps you wake up with stiff, aching joints that make even the most basic movements difficult. Perhaps your energy drops in the mid-afternoon, leaving you too exhausted to enjoy life. Perhaps your digestion is unpredictable, resulting in bloating, discomfort, or unexplained gut issues that appear out of nowhere. You might even be dealing with stubborn weight gain, brain fog, or persistent headaches, and nothing seems to work.

If any of this sounds familiar, you aren't alone. 3 out of 5 people worldwide suffer from chronic inflammation, which contributes to conditions such as heart disease, diabetes, arthritis, and even depression (World Health Organization). It's been dubbed the "silent killer" because it doesn't present with obvious symptoms at first. Instead, it builds gradually, like an invisible fire in your body, burning beneath the surface and eroding your health.

This is something I know firsthand.

For years, I ignored the warning signs: occasional joint pain, skin flare-ups, and digestive discomfort. I attributed it to "getting older" or "stress." But then things worsened. My energy levels plummeted, my brain felt sluggish, and I found myself relying on caffeine and sugar to get through the day. Doctors conducted tests, but nothing was "technically wrong." I was told that it was just part of life.

But deep down, I knew something wasn't right.

That's when I realized the connection between food and inflammation—and everything changed.

What If Your Food Is Causing You Pain?

Here's the harsh reality: Much of what we eat today is making us sick. The modern diet contains processed foods, excess sugar, unhealthy fats, and hidden additives, all of which cause chronic inflammation in the body. What are the consequences?

- Joint pain, stiffness, and autoimmune flare-ups
- Unrelenting weight gain
- Constant bloating, gas, or digestive distress
- Migraines, brain fog, and difficulty focusing

- Fatigue that persists even after a full night's sleep
- Skin conditions such as acne, eczema, or

Sounds familiar?

This is more than just an inconvenience; it is a serious warning sign. Your body is indicating that something isn't working. And ignoring it may lead to bigger problems in the future, such as heart disease, Alzheimer's, or even cancer. The Lancet, 2020 reports that chronic inflammation is linked to 50% of all deaths worldwide.

But here's some good news: You have the ability to stop it.

The Anti-Inflammatory Diet

When I first heard the term "anti-inflammatory diet," I thought it was just a fad. But this is not about counting calories, starving yourself, or adhering to impossible rules. It is about giving your body the nutrients it requires to heal and removing the foods that feed the fire of inflammation.

According to scientific research, an anti-inflammatory diet can alleviate pain, increase energy, improve digestion, and even prevent chronic disease. In one study, participants who switched to an anti-inflammatory diet experienced a 37% reduction in joint pain and a 50% decrease in fatigue within weeks (Arthritis Foundation).

- Consider waking up without stiff joints.
- Imagine feeling energized rather than exhausted by noon.
- Imagine eating meals that not only taste great but heal your body from the inside out.

That is what this book is about.

How This Book Will Transform Your Life

I wrote this book because I understand what it's like to be stuck, frustrated, and exhausted. I understand what it's like to try every diet, supplement, and "hack" and still feel like nothing works. I also understand what it feels like to finally find a solution that actually works.

Within these pages, you will find:

✓ The real science behind inflammation—how it works and how to stop it
✓ The worst foods for inflammation (and the surprising ones that may be harming you)
✓ The best anti-inflammatory foods—what to eat and why they work
✓ A step-by-step elimination plan to identify your personal trigger foods
✓ Simple, delicious recipes that nourish your body and fight inflammation

- ✓ Practical lifestyle changes to reduce stress, improve sleep, and

This is not about perfection. It is about progress. It is about making small, long-term changes that will have a significant impact on your health and quality of life.

You do not have to live with chronic pain, fatigue, or digestive problems. You do not have to accept brain fog or mood swings as "just a part of getting older." And you don't have to keep guessing about which foods are good or bad for you.

If you're ready to feel better, think more clearly, and regain your energy, let's get started. Your journey to an inflammation-free life begins right now.

CHAPTER 1

THE ANTI-INFLAMMATORY DIET: WHAT YOU SHOULD KNOW

Dear Friend,

If you're still reading this, you're probably dealing with chronic pain, fatigue, or some mysterious illness that doctors can't explain—or maybe you're just tired of feeling "off" all the time. I get it. I have been there, too. I spent years attributing my aches and brain fog to "just getting older" or "stress." But the truth is that I was inflamed. I didn't even realize it.

The term "inflammation" is frequently used, usually in reference to disease. But what if I told you that inflammation isn't necessarily bad? In fact, it's your body's natural defense system, designed to protect you. What's the problem? In our modern world, this once-beneficial system is being hijacked—by the very foods we eat.

Let us break it down.

What is inflammation, really?

Imagine you've cut your finger. Your body responds almost instantly: white blood cells rush to the scene, blood vessels expand, and you may experience redness, swelling, or even warmth. This is acute inflammation, your body's method of healing and fighting infection. This is a good thing.

Imagine this process taking place inside your body all the time, even when there is no injury to heal. That is chronic inflammation, which is an entirely different beast. Chronic inflammation, unlike a swollen finger that heals in a few days, lingers beneath the surface for months or years, causing damage to tissues, joints, and even organs.

Chronic inflammation is primarily caused by an overactive immune response. Your body mistakenly perceives threats where none exist, releasing a steady stream of pro-inflammatory molecules such as cytokines and prostaglandins. This ongoing immune activation may contribute to diseases like:

- Heart disease (Inflammation damages arteries, causing plaque buildup.)
- Diabetes (Inflammatory compounds inhibit insulin signaling)
- Arthritis (Joint inflammation causes pain and stiffness.)
- Alzheimer's disease (Chronic inflammation promotes brain plaque formation).
- Autoimmune Disorders (The immune system attacks its own tissues.)

And here's the kicker: one of the leading causes of chronic inflammation is right on our plates.

How Food Fuels The Fire

Our ancestors consumed whole, unprocessed foods straight from nature. Today? We eat highly processed, sugary, chemically altered foods that confuse and overwhelm our bodies. What happens when we consistently eat inflammatory foods?

- Blood sugar spikes: High-glycemic foods (such as white bread, pastries, and soda) cause insulin surges, resulting in inflammation.
- Damaged fats: Trans fats and excessive omega-6 fatty acids (found in vegetable oils) raise inflammatory markers in the blood.
- Leaky gut syndrome: Additives, sugar, and gluten can damage the gut lining, allowing toxins and bacteria to enter the bloodstream and cause widespread inflammation.

What's the outcome? Chronic pain, fatigue, mental fog, digestive problems, and an increased risk of chronic disease.

Anti-Inflammatory Diet: Your Natural Defence System

Now for the good news: some foods trigger inflammation, while others calm it down. The anti-inflammatory diet is not about deprivation; it is about eating foods that work with your body, not against it.

The foods we eat have a direct impact on our bodies' inflammatory pathways. According to research, polyphenols, antioxidants, and healthy fats can help combat chronic inflammation at the cellular level. Here's how.

- Omega-3 fatty acids (found in fatty fish, flaxseeds, and walnuts) inhibit the production of pro-inflammatory molecules such as leukotrienes and prostaglandins.
- Polyphenols (found in berries, green tea, and dark chocolate) lower oxidative stress and protect cells from damage.
- Curcumin (the active compound in turmeric) inhibits inflammatory enzymes, much like some anti-inflammatory drugs.

✓ Fiber-rich foods (such as leafy greens, legumes, and whole grains) promote gut health by keeping harmful bacteria from causing inflammation.

What to Eat (and Avoid)

These foods have been scientifically proven to reduce inflammation:

✓ Fatty Fish (salmon, sardines, mackerel) - Omega-3s reduce inflammation.
✓ Berries (blueberries, strawberries, raspberries) - Antioxidants combat oxidative stress.
✓ Leafy greens, Spinach, kale, and Swiss chard are high in polyphenols and fiber.
✓ Nuts and seeds: Walnuts, flaxseeds, and chia seeds are excellent sources of anti-inflammatory fats.
✓ Olive Oil contains oleocanthal, which has ibuprofen-like effects.
✓ Turmeric & Ginger are natural anti-inflammatory spices with powerful healing properties.
✓ Green Tea contains catechins that reduce inflammation and improve brain health.

Inflammatory Offenders

These foods promote chronic inflammation and should be limited or avoided:

- Refined Carbs (white bread, pasta, pastries) can cause blood sugar spikes and increase inflammatory cytokines.
- Sugar and artificial sweeteners can disrupt metabolism and increase insulin resistance.
- Processed Meats (such as sausages, hot dogs, and deli meats) contain harmful preservatives and inflammatory compounds.
- Trans Fats & Vegetable Oils (Margarine, soybean oil, canola oil) can increase inflammation and oxidative stress.
- Excessive Alcohol weakens the gut lining, allowing toxins into the bloodstream.

Is the Anti-Inflammatory Diet Really Effective?

The proof is in the results. According to research, people who consume an anti-inflammatory diet experience:

- Reduced joint pain - especially for arthritis patients.
- Improved gut health - Reduces the risk of IBS and leaky gut.
- Better heart health - Lower cholesterol and less plaque buildup in arteries.
- Enhanced brain function - Reduced brain fog and a lower risk of neurodegenerative diseases.
- Balanced weight - Reduced bloating, more consistent energy levels, and easier weight management.

Personally, when I made the transition, I noticed something profound: my energy returned. The brain fog had lifted. What about my chronic aches? Gone. It felt like I had rebooted my body, giving it the energy it had been craving all along.

What you put on your plate conveys a message to your body. It can say either:

"Let's heal."

Or...

"Let's inflame."

The choice is yours. You don't have to completely overhaul your diet overnight, but even minor changes can have a significant impact. Begin by swapping inflammatory foods for anti-inflammatory alternatives. Listen to your body. Pay attention to your feelings.

Your health is more than just what you avoid; it is also about what you nourish your body with. The power to heal is already within you. Now all you need to do is feed it.

CHAPTER 2

HOW TO EAT THE ANTI-INFLAMMATORY WAY

If you've ever looked at a plate of food and wondered, is this helping or hurting me? You're not alone. Most of us have been conditioned to eat for taste, convenience, or habit, but we rarely consider whether our meals are beneficial to our health or causing inflammation.

Learning to eat anti-inflammatory isn't about strict diets, calorie counting, or avoiding all indulgences. It's about making deliberate choices—eating foods that nourish, heal, and work with your body, not against it. Vegetables and greens are among the most effective healing foods.

Let's look at why greens are such powerful anti-inflammatory foods, how to choose the best ones, and how to prepare them for maximum benefit.

If you had to choose just one type of food to consume more of for anti-inflammatory benefits, vegetables—particularly leafy greens—should be at the top of the list. They are packed with essential nutrients that combat inflammation at the cellular level.

The Science of Greens and Inflammation

Vegetables, especially dark leafy greens, contain

- Antioxidants: These compounds neutralize free radicals, which cause oxidative stress and chronic inflammation.
- Polyphenols are plant compounds that actively reduce inflammatory markers in the body.
- Fiber - Promotes gut health by reducing inflammatory gut bacteria and regulating blood sugar.
- Vitamins & Minerals - Examples include vitamin C (reduces inflammation), magnesium (calms the nervous system), and folate (helps with detoxification).

Research has shown that people who consume more leafy greens have lower levels of C-reactive protein (CRP), a key marker of inflammation associated with heart disease, arthritis, and autoimmune conditions.

How to Select the Best Greens

Not all greens are made equal. While all vegetables have benefits, some have a stronger anti-inflammatory effect. When choosing greens, look for nutrient density and low pesticide exposure.

- ✓ Kale is a nutrient-dense green that contains vitamin K, beta-carotene, and polyphenols that reduce inflammation
- ✓ Spinach contains quercetin, a flavonoid with powerful anti-inflammatory properties.
- ✓ Swiss Chard has unique antioxidants that reduce oxidative stress and inflammation
- ✓ Collard greens high in fiber and sulfur compounds, which aid in liver detoxification.
- ✓ Arugula contains glucosinolates, which regulate the body's inflammation response.
- ✓ Microgreens contain up to 40 times more nutrients than mature greens.
- ✓ Seaweed is a lesser-known green that contains fucoxanthin, an antioxidant that fights inflammation at a cellular level.

What to Avoid When Selecting Greens

- Iceberg lettuce is not harmful, but lacks the nutrient density of darker greens.
- Non-organic leafy greens - Conventional greens are frequently sprayed with pesticides, which can exacerbate inflammation. If organic isn't an option, thoroughly clean with vinegar and water to remove residue.
- Greens were stored for too long Greens lose nutrients as they sit in the fridge for an extended period of time. Buy fresh and eat within a few days for the best results.

How to Prepare Greens Anti-Inflammatory Way

Once you've decided on your greens, how you prepare them can make all the difference. The incorrect cooking methods can deplete their healing properties, whereas the proper methods can amplify their anti-inflammatory benefits.

<u>Use raw in salads and smoothies</u>

- ∗ Maintains high antioxidant and polyphenol levels.
- ∗ The best greens for raw consumption are spinach, kale, arugula, and microgreens.

Tip: Add a healthy fat (such as olive oil or avocado) to improve nutrient absorption.

<u>Lightly Steamed</u>

- ∗ Preserves nutrients and makes greens easier to digest
- ∗ Best with kale, Swiss chard, and collard greens.

Tip: Steam for only 3-5 minutes to protect vitamin C and antioxidants.

<u>Sautéed in healthy fats</u>

- ∗ Facilitates the absorption of fat-soluble vitamins (A, D, E, and K).
- ∗ Ideal for: spinach, kale, collard greens, and mustard greens.

Tip: Use anti-inflammatory fats such as olive oil, avocado oil, and ghee. Avoid vegetable oils!

<u>Fermented (Kimchi, Sauerkraut)</u>

- Promotes gut health by introducing beneficial probiotics.
- Best with cabbage, mustard greens, and kale.

Tip: Purchase raw, unpasteurized versions or make your own at home.

<u>Incorporated into soups and pestos</u>

- A healthy way to consume greens in warm dishes without overcooking.
- Best for spinach, basil, and kale.

Tip: Add greens near the end of cooking to preserve nutrients.

Common Mistakes That Can Decrease Anti-Inflammatory Benefits

- Boiling Greens for Too Long - Water-soluble vitamins, such as vitamin C and folate, leach into the water. If you must boil, use the water for soups or broths.
- Cooking in Vegetable Oils on High Heat Oils such as canola, soybean, and sunflower oil are high in omega-6 fatty acids, which promote inflammation. Stick with olive oil, coconut oil, or avocado oil.
- Eating Greens without Healthy Fats: Fat-soluble vitamins (A, D, E, K) require fat for absorption. Always pair greens with healthy fats, such as olive oil, nuts, seeds, or avocado.
- Overload with Raw Kale or Spinach: While raw greens are extremely nutritious, consuming too much raw kale or spinach can impair thyroid function due to their goitrogenic compounds. If you have thyroid issues, lightly steaming these greens is ideal.

Make Greens a Daily Habit

Now that you've learned how to choose and prepare anti-inflammatory greens, the next step is to incorporate them into your daily routine. Here are some simple ways to accomplish that:

- ✓ Begin your day with a green smoothie (mix spinach, avocado, banana, and almond milk for a powerhouse drink).
- ✓ Incorporate greens into every meal (toss arugula into scrambled eggs, mix kale into soups, or top sandwiches with microgreens).
- ✓ Snack on veggie chips (create your own by baking kale or Swiss chard with olive oil and sea salt).
- ✓ Use greens as wraps (Collard greens are an excellent substitute for tortillas and sandwich bread).
- ✓ Make a large batch of sautéed greens (store in the fridge and use in meals throughout the week).

The goal of anti-inflammatory eating is not perfection, but rather progress. When you choose greens over processed foods, olive oil over vegetable oil, or whole foods over packaged ones, you are sending a powerful message to your body.

Nom Nom your Way to not Feeling like Garbage | **Irene Fields**

I chose healing.

Your body is constantly listening. When given the appropriate fuel, it knows exactly what to do. So start small, be consistent, and see how even the simplest changes, such as eating more greens, can improve your energy, health, and vitality.

Omega-3 Fatty Acids

If there is one nutrient that deserves a gold medal for fighting inflammation, it is omega-3 fatty acids. They're like tiny peacekeepers, working behind the scenes to reduce your body's inflammation response. However, most of us don't get nearly enough of them.

You've probably heard of omega-3s before—perhaps in relation to fish oil supplements or heart health. But their impact extends far beyond that. They affect brain function, joint health, gut balance, and mood regulation. More importantly, they directly combat the effects of chronic inflammation, which is at the heart of many modern diseases.

Let's go over what omega-3s do, how they combat inflammation, and how you can easily incorporate them into your daily routine.

Anti-Inflammatory Properties of Omega-3s

Inflammation is your body's natural defense mechanism, helping to fight infections and heal injuries. However, when inflammation lingers (due to poor diet, stress, and environmental toxins), it becomes a silent threat, contributing to conditions such as arthritis, heart disease, autoimmune disorders, and depression.

This is where omega-3s come in. These are essential fats:

- Reduce Inflammatory Cytokines: Cytokines are signaling molecules that cause inflammation. Omega-3s actively inhibit the production of pro-inflammatory cytokines such as IL-6 and TNF-alpha.
- Lower CRP - High CRP levels are a strong indicator of chronic inflammation. Studies have shown that omega-3s can significantly reduce CRP levels, lowering the risk of heart disease and metabolic disorders.
- Boosts Brain and Mood Health - Inflammation is associated with depression, anxiety, and cognitive decline, in addition to being harmful to the body itself. Omega-3s, particularly DHA, are essential for brain function and have been shown to alleviate symptoms of anxiety and depression.
- Balanced Omega-6 to Omega-3 Ratio: The modern Western diet contains a lot of inflammatory omega-6 fats. Omega-3s help to rebalance this ratio, thereby preventing chronic inflammation.

- Safeguard Joint and Heart Health - Omega-3 fatty acids act as a natural lubricant for joints, alleviating arthritis symptoms and joint pain. They also lower triglycerides, increase blood flow, and keep arteries flexible, lowering the risk of heart disease.

How I Incorporate Omega-3s into My Daily Life

Now that we understand why omega-3s are so effective, the next question is how do we get enough of them?

Our bodies cannot produce omega-3s on their own, so we must obtain them through food or supplements. Here's how I ensure I get my daily dose of anti-inflammatory goodness.

1. Consuming Fatty Fish Regularly

Fatty fish are excellent sources of omega-3s. I attempt to include at least two servings per week of:
- Salmon is one of the richest sources of EPA and DHA.
- Mackerel (rich in omega-3s and vitamin D).
- Sardines (affordable, sustainable, and rich in nutrients)
- Herring (an excellent mild-flavored choice)
- Anchovies (ideal for salads and homemade dressings)

How to do it:
- Bake or pan-sear salmon with olive oil, lemon, and herbs.
- Add sardines or mackerel to salads for a protein-rich boost.
- Prepare a simple anchovy-garlic dressing for roasted vegetables.

2. Introducing Plant-Based Omega-3s

While plant-based sources do not contain EPA & DHA, they do provide ALA (alpha-linolenic acid), which the body can convert (albeit inefficiently). Still, I enjoy incorporating these sources for additional support:

- Chia Seeds (full of fiber and omega-3s)
- Flaxseeds (excellent for gut health and hormonal balance)
- Walnuts (high in ALA and polyphenols, which reduce oxidative stress)
- Hemp Seeds (good balance of omega-3 and omega-6)

How I Do It:
- Add a tablespoon of chia seeds to my morning smoothie.
- Sprinkle ground flaxseeds on oatmeal, yogurt, or salad.
- Enjoy a handful of walnuts in the afternoon.
- Sprinkle hemp seeds on avocado toast for an extra omega-3 boost.

3. Cooking with Omega-3 Rich Oils

Nom Nom your Way to not Feeling like Garbage | **Irene Fields**

Most people cook with inflammatory vegetable oils (such as soybean, corn, or sunflower oil), which contain high levels of omega-6s. I make an intentional effort to **replace** these with healthier oils:

- Extra Virgin Olive Oil
- While low in omega-3s, it contains potent polyphenols that fight inflammation.
- Avocado Oil - A heart-healthy fat with an optimal omega ratio.
- Flaxseed Oil - A plant-based omega-3 powerhouse (best drizzled, not cooked).

How I do it:
- Drizzle flaxseed oil on salads or roast vegetables.
- Use olive oil for dressings, marinades, and low-temperature cooking.
- Use avocado oil for higher-heat frying or roasting.

4. Consuming High-Quality Omega-3 Supplements

Even with the best diet, I occasionally fall short of omega-3s—so I supplement. Not all fish oils are made equal, so I look for:

- ✓ Molecularly distilled to eliminate heavy metals
- ✓ High EPA & DHA content (at least 1,000mg per serving)
- ✓ Sustainably sourced (from wild-caught fish)

How I do it:
* Take 1,000-2,000mg of high-quality fish oil daily, especially on days when I do not consume fish.
* If I need a plant-based alternative, I use algal oil, which is high in DHA.

5. Reduced Omega-6 Intake

It's not just about adding omega-3s; it's also about reducing omega-6s, which cause inflammation when consumed in excess. I avoid:

- Processed vegetable oils (canola, corn, soybean, sunflower)
- Fried and processed foods
- Excess grain-fed meats (with low omega-6 to omega-3 ratio)

Instead, I stick to grass-fed meats, wild fish, and whole foods.

When I first started focusing on omega-3s, I had low expectations. Within weeks, I noticed:
- ✓ Reduced joint stiffness
- ✓ Increased mental clarity
- ✓ Improved mood and focus
- ✓ Healthier skin (no dry patches!)
- ✓ Reduced bloating and digestive discomfort.

It's a small but significant change. You don't have to change your diet overnight—just start small:
- Include a handful of walnuts in your breakfast.
- Replace inflammatory oils with olive or avocado oil.
- This week, enjoy a piece of grilled salmon.

Fermented Foods, Gut Health, and Inflammation

Let's talk about something that may surprise you: your gut.

Most people associate inflammation with sore joints, puffiness, and even chronic diseases such as arthritis. But what if I told you that most of your body's inflammation begins in your gut?

Your digestive system contains trillions of bacteria, fungi, and microbes, collectively known as the gut microbiome. These microscopic organisms do more than just help you digest food; they also regulate immunity, inflammation, and even mood and brain function.

If your gut is healthy, your body thrives. Is it inflamed and unbalanced? This is when things go wrong.

Consuming fermented foods is one of the simplest ways to maintain gut health and reduce inflammation. These probiotic-rich powerhouses aid in the rebuilding and maintenance of a robust, diverse microbiome, thereby reducing inflammation at its source.

Let's look at how it all works and how you can begin incorporating fermented foods into your daily routine.

Gut Health and Inflammation: What's the Link?

Imagine your gut is a fortress. Inside, an army of beneficial bacteria keeps everything in check, ensuring that only good stuff is absorbed and harmful invaders are kept out.

But here's the issue: Modern life—processed foods, sugar, antibiotics, stress, and environmental toxins—weakens this fortress, killing off the good bacteria and allowing harmful ones to take over.

When this happens, you get:

- Leaky Gut (Intestinal Permeability): Damage to the gut lining allows toxins and undigested food particles to enter the bloodstream, leading to widespread inflammation.
- Dysbiosis (Imbalanced Gut Bacteria) - When harmful bacteria outnumber beneficial bacteria, it causes bloating, digestive issues, and an overactive immune response, which fuels chronic inflammation.
- Overactive Immune System - With 70% of immune cells in the gut, an unhealthy microbiome can cause the immune system to attack healthy cells, potentially leading to autoimmune diseases.

Here's where fermented foods come in.

Anti-inflammatory Properties of Fermented Foods

Fermented foods contain probiotics, which help replenish beneficial gut bacteria and restore balance. This, in turn, reduces inflammation and boosts overall health. Here's how.

- ✓ Strengthens the Gut Barrier: Fermented foods contain probiotics that repair the gut lining and prevent harmful toxins from entering the bloodstream.
- ✓ Reduces Chronic Inflammation - A healthy microbiome generates short-chain fatty acids (SCFAs), such as butyrate, which actively lower inflammatory markers in the body.
- ✓ Regulates the Immune System: Healthy gut bacteria train immune cells to respond appropriately, reducing autoimmune flare-ups and inflammation.
- ✓ Balances Blood Sugar and Metabolism - Fermented foods can help regulate blood sugar levels, which is important as high blood sugar spikes can cause inflammation.
- ✓ Boosts brain and mood health - The gut-brain axis connects the gut and the brain. A healthy microbiome lowers stress, anxiety, and brain fog, all of which are associated with inflammation.

How I Use Fermented Foods in My Daily Life

Now that we understand why fermented foods are so beneficial, the question is: How do we incorporate them into our diet in an easy and sustainable manner?

This is what I do.

1. Sauerkraut, a Gut-Healing Superfood
Sauerkraut (fermented cabbage), one of the simplest and most inexpensive fermented foods, contains probiotics, vitamin C, and digestive enzymes.

How I do it:
- Use a spoonful in salads, grain bowls, or wraps.
- Serve it as a side to roasted meats or grilled fish.
- Have a bite before meals to help digestion.

2. Kimchi, the Spicy Inflammation Fighter
Kimchi, a Korean staple, is made by fermenting cabbage, radishes, and spices. It contains probiotics, antioxidants, and anti-inflammatory compounds.

How I do it:
- Add it to scrambled eggs or omelets.
- Add it to soups, stews, or stir-fries for a probiotic boost.
- Serve as a topping on avocado toast or tacos.

3. Kefir is a probiotic powerhouse
Kefir is a fermented dairy (or nondairy) beverage that contains more probiotics than yogurt. It is excellent for improving digestion and reducing bloating.

How I do it:
- Blend it into smoothies.
- Use it as the foundation for salad dressings.
- Drink a small glass in the morning to start your day with probiotics.

4. Miso, the Gut-Friendly Seasoning
Miso is a fermented soybean paste commonly used in Japanese cuisine. It's packed with probiotics, enzymes, and antioxidants.

How I do it:
- Stir it into soups (but don't boil it, as high heat kills probiotics!).
- Use it in marinades for fish, chicken, and vegetables.
- Make a simple miso-tahini dressing for salads.

5. Tempeh: Protein-Rich Fermented Food
Tempeh is a fermented soybean product high in probiotics and plant-based protein. It also contains compounds that decrease oxidative stress.

How I do it:
- Sauté with garlic, turmeric, and olive oil for a simple anti-inflammatory meal.
- Mix it into stir-fries or grain bowls.
- Serve it as a meat substitute in tacos or sandwiches.

6. Yogurt: The Classic Probiotic Food
High-quality, plain, unsweetened yogurt contains live active cultures that promote gut health.

How I do it:
- Add berries, flaxseeds, and honey.
- Use it as the foundation for tzatziki sauce or probiotic-rich dips.
- Add a dollop to spicy dishes to cool them down and improve gut health.

When I first started eating fermented foods, I had low expectations. Within a few weeks, I experienced:

- ✓ Less bloating and digestive discomfort
- ✓ Better energy levels
- ✓ Clearer skin
- ✓ Less brain fog and mood swings
- ✓ Fewer sugar cravings.

And the best part? I didn't have to make drastic changes. Simply adding a spoonful of sauerkraut here, a glass of kefir there—it all added up.

So, if you're looking for an easy, natural way to reduce inflammation, start here. Your gut is the gateway to your health, and eating the right foods makes all the difference.

Herbs and Spices That Heal

If you're like me, you probably don't want to completely change your diet overnight. But what if I told you that one of the simplest ways to fight inflammation is as easy as opening your spice cabinet?

Herbs and spices aren't just for flavor; they're also some of the world's most powerful anti-inflammatory foods. For thousands of years, cultures all over the world have used them not only to flavor food, but also as medicine. And modern science is finally catching up, demonstrating that these small but powerful ingredients can help reduce inflammation, improve digestion, balance blood sugar, and even protect against chronic diseases.

So, let's look at the best anti-inflammatory herbs and spices and how to easily incorporate them into your meals.

Why Are Herbs and Spices So Powerful?

Inflammation occurs when the body produces chemicals such as cytokines and prostaglandins in response to an injury, stress, or infection. While short-term inflammation is required for healing, chronic inflammation—caused by poor diet, stress, or environmental toxins—can lead to diseases such as arthritis, heart disease, diabetes, and even Alzheimer's.

The good news is that certain herbs and spices contain potent compounds that naturally reduce inflammation by blocking inflammatory pathways and neutralizing free radicals.

1. Turmeric: Curcumin is the key compound.

Turmeric is undoubtedly one of the most researched anti-inflammatory spices. Its active ingredient, curcumin, has been shown to block inflammatory markers such as NF-kB, which is associated with chronic diseases. Curcumin has been shown in studies to be as effective as some anti-inflammatory drugs—without the side effects!

How do I use it?
✓ I add a teaspoon to smoothies with black pepper (to increase absorption).
✓ I add it to soups, stews, and scrambled eggs.

Nom Nom your Way to not Feeling like Garbage | **Irene Fields**

✓ I prepare turmeric tea (golden milk) using warm almond milk, cinnamon, and honey.

2. Ginger: Key Compound: Gingerol

Ginger is nature's ibuprofen, reducing pain, stiffness, and inflammation by inhibiting COX-2 enzymes (the same enzymes that painkillers target). According to research, it can help with arthritis, muscle pain, and even digestive issues such as bloating.

How do I use it?
✓ I add grated fresh ginger to hot tea or lemon water.
✓ I use it in stir-fries, curries, and salad dressings.
✓ I add it to smoothies to boost their anti-inflammatory benefits.

3. Cinnamon: Key Compound: Cinnamaldehyde

Cinnamon is a powerful anti-inflammatory spice that lowers blood sugar, improves insulin sensitivity, and reduces oxidative stress. Because high blood sugar causes inflammation, cinnamon is an excellent daily supplement

How do I use it?
✓ I sprinkle it on oatmeal, yogurt, and coffee.
✓ I add it to homemade energy balls with nuts and dates.
✓ I use a dash in smoothies and baked goods.

4. Garlic: Allicin is the key compound.

Garlic is a natural remedy that reduces inflammation, fights infections, and promotes heart health. It contains allicin, which has been shown to reduce inflammation markers such as CRP and TNF-alpha.

How do I use it?
✓ I crush fresh garlic and let it sit for 10 minutes to boost its allicin content.
✓ I use it in soups, sauces, roasted vegetables, and dressings.
✓ I sometimes eat a raw clove in the morning (it's strong, but it works wonders!).

5. Rosemary: Key Compound: Rosmarinic Acid

Rosemary is high in antioxidants that reduce inflammation in the brain, which helps with memory, focus, and even Alzheimer's prevention. It also boosts circulation and aids digestion.

How do I use it?
✓ I add it to olive oil for cooking.
✓ I add it to roasted vegetables, fish, and chicken.

✓ I make rosemary tea for a cognitive boost.

6. Oregano: Key Compound

Carvacrol Oregano is a potent anti-inflammatory and antimicrobial herb, rich in antioxidants that fight infections and support immune health.

How do I use it?
✓ I add dried oregano to salads, soups, and roasted vegetables.
✓ I incorporate fresh oregano into homemade pesto.
✓ I use diluted oregano oil for cold and flu relief.

7. Cayenne Pepper: Key Compound: Capsaicin

Cayenne pepper contains capsaicin, which reduces inflammation and blocks pain signals, making it effective against arthritis and muscle pain.

How do I use it?
✓ I use a pinch in spicy dishes, soups, and stir-fries.
✓ I add it to hot lemon water for a metabolism boost.
✓ I use cayenne-infused oil for muscle and joint pain.

8. Cloves: Key Compound: Eugenol Cloves contain more antioxidants than almost any other spice and aid in pain relief, digestion, and inflammation reduction.

How do I use it?
✓ I add ground cloves to chai tea and baked goods.
✓ I use whole cloves when making homemade broth or curry.
I chew a clove when I feel a sore throat coming on.

How to Add More Herbs and Spices to Your Diet

1. Spice up your breakfast - Sprinkle cinnamon on oatmeal, ginger on smoothies, or turmeric on scrambled eggs.
2. Add flavor to your water - Infuse it with fresh mint, ginger, or rosemary.
3. Upgrade your tea - Use turmeric, ginger, or cinnamon tea instead of sugary beverages.
4. Boost your salads - Add fresh basil, cilantro, or oregano to dressings and toppings.
5. Improve your cooking - Mix garlic, rosemary, and cayenne into roasted vegetables, meats, or soups.
6. Make your own spice blends - Make a homemade anti-inflammatory blend with turmeric, black pepper, cinnamon, and ginger.

Nom Nom your Way to not Feeling like Garbage | **Irene Fields**

When I started incorporating more herbs and spices into my daily meals, I wasn't expecting to feel the difference so quickly. However, within weeks, I noticed:

- Reduced joint pain and stiffness
- Improved digestion and bloating
- Increased energy and clarity
- Improved immune function

The best part? It's so simple. You don't have to change your entire diet—just sprinkle, sip, and stir your way to better health.

BREAKFAST AND FIRST MEALS

Nom Nom your Way to not Feeling like Garbage | **Irene Fields**

Spinach & Egg Scramble

Prep Time: 5 minutes

Cook Time: 5 minutes

Servings: 1 (about 1 ½ cups of scramble)

2 large pasture-raised eggs

1 cup fresh spinach, roughly chopped

1 tbsp extra virgin olive oil

¼ tsp turmeric powder

1 small garlic clove, minced

2 tbsp unsweetened almond milk

Pinch of black pepper (helps activate turmeric!)

Pinch of sea salt

Optional toppings: sliced avocado, microgreens, or a sprinkle of hemp seeds

Pro Tips & Variations:

Make it dairy-free? Skip the almond milk—it's just for fluff.

Add extra protein? Add smoked salmon or cooked quinoa.

Spice it up? Add a pinch of cayenne or red pepper flakes.

More greens? Swap spinach with kale, Swiss chard, or arugula.

1. Heat it up

In a nonstick pan, heat the olive oil over medium heat. Add the minced garlic and sauté for 30 seconds, until fragrant.

2. Wilt the spinach. Cook the chopped spinach for 1 minute, stirring occasionally, until softened but still vibrant green.

3. In a bowl, whisk together the eggs, almond milk, turmeric, black pepper, and sea salt until well combined.

4. Scramble time

Pour the eggs over the spinach and allow to sit for 10 seconds before gently stirring with a spatula. Cook for about 2-3 minutes, stirring occasionally, until just set.

5. Plate and enjoy.

Transfer to a plate and garnish with avocado, microgreens, or hemp seeds for an added boost!

Nom Nom your Way to not Feeling like Garbage | **Irene Fields**

Avocado & Kale Omelet

Prep Time: 5 minutes

Cook Time: 7 minutes

Servings: 1 (makes one 8-inch omelet)

Pro Tips & Variations:

Add toasted pumpkin seeds for extra crunch.

Make it dairy-free? Instead of feta, use nutritional yeast.

For extra protein, add smoked salmon or shredded chicken.

Add a spicy twist. Add some red pepper flakes or a dash of hot sauce.

2 large pasture-raised eggs

1 tbsp unsweetened almond milk

½ cup kale, finely chopped

½ small avocado, sliced

1 tbsp extra virgin olive oil

¼ tsp turmeric powder

Pinch of black pepper

Pinch of sea salt

Optional extras: crumbled feta, cherry tomatoes, red pepper flakes

1. Whisk the eggs.

In a mixing bowl, combine the eggs, almond milk, turmeric, black pepper, and sea salt until thoroughly combined.

2. Sauté the kale with olive oil in a nonstick pan over medium heat. Add the kale and cook for 1-2 minutes, until slightly wilted but still bright green

3. Cook the omelet. Lower the heat to medium-low, add the egg mixture, and swirl to distribute evenly. Allow it to cook undisturbed for 3-4 minutes, until the edges begin to set.

4. Fill and Fold.

Layer on avocado slices (and feta or tomatoes, if using). Gently fold the omelet in half and cook for an additional 30 seconds to heat through.

5. Serve and enjoy.

Slide onto a plate, garnish with extra avocado if desired, and dig in

Nom Nom your Way to not Feeling like Garbage | **Irene Fields**

Egg Salad Avocado Toast

Prep Time: 10 minutes

Cook Time: 10 minutes (for boiling eggs)

Servings: 1 (makes 1 loaded slice of toast)

Pro Tip & Variation:

For extra crunch, add chopped celery or radishes.

For extra protein, add smoked salmon or hemp seeds.

Low-carb option: Serve egg salad in lettuce cups instead of bread.

Want a spicy kick? Add a little cayenne or sriracha.

1 slice whole-grain or sourdough bread

2 hard-boiled eggs, chopped

½ small avocado, mashed

1 tbsp extra virgin olive oil

½ tsp Dijon mustard

¼ tsp turmeric powder

Pinch of black pepper

Pinch of sea salt

1 tsp lemon juice

Toppings (optional): microgreens, red pepper flakes, hemp seeds

1. To boil eggs, place them in cold water, bring to a boil, and simmer for 10 minutes. Transfer to an ice bath, then peel and chop.

2. To prepare the creamy mix, mash the avocado with olive oil, Dijon mustard, turmeric, black pepper, sea salt, and lemon juice until smooth.

3. Fold in the chopped eggs into the avocado mixture until thoroughly combined.

4. While the egg salad sits, toast the bread until golden and crisp.

5. Spread the egg salad generously on the toast. Add microgreens, red pepper flakes, or hemp seeds for an extra nutritional boost.

Nom Nom your Way to not Feeling like Garbage | **Irene Fields**

Smoked Salmon & Omelet

Prep Time: 5 minutes

Cook Time: 7 minutes

Servings: 1 (makes one 8-inch omelet)

Pro Tips & Variations:

Dairy-free? Skip the almond milk—it's just for fluffiness.

Want extra greens? Add a handful of sautéed spinach or arugula.

Spicy? Add red pepper flakes or hot sauce.

If you don't have smoked salmon, substitute canned wild-caught salmon or grilled shrimp.

- 2 large pasture-raised eggs
- 1 tbsp unsweetened almond milk
- 2 oz smoked salmon, torn into pieces
- ½ tsp extra virgin olive oil
- ¼ tsp turmeric powder
- Pinch of black pepper
- Pinch of sea salt
- Toppings (optional): sliced avocado, fresh dill, capers, red onion slices

1. In a mixing bowl, combine the eggs, almond milk, turmeric, black pepper, and sea salt. Beat until smooth.

2. Warm olive oil in a nonstick pan on medium-low heat.

3. Cook the omelet. Pour in the egg mixture and cook for 3-4 minutes without stirring until the edges set.

4. Once the omelet is mostly set but slightly soft on top, spread the smoked salmon evenly over one half.

5. Gently fold the omelet in half and cook for an additional 30 seconds to warm through.

6. Transfer to a plate and garnish with sliced avocado, fresh dill, or capers for added flavor!

Nom Nom your Way to not Feeling like Garbage | **Irene Fields**

Southwestern Waffle with Eggs

Prep Time: 10 minutes

Cook Time: 5 minutes

Servings: 1 (makes 1 large waffle with toppings)

Pro Tips & Variations:

To make it spicier, add diced jalapeños to the batter or top with hot sauce.

For more protein, add shredded chicken or smoked salmon.

Don't have a waffle iron? Use a nonstick pan to make a pancake.

Dairy-free option? This already exists! However, nutritional yeast can be added to give the dish a cheesy flavor.

For the Waffle:

½ cup almond flour

1 tbsp ground flaxseed

½ tsp baking powder

¼ tsp turmeric powder

¼ tsp cumin

Pinch of sea salt

1 large pasture-raised egg

¼ cup unsweetened almond milk

½ tbsp extra virgin olive oil

Toppings:

1 large pasture-raised egg, fried or poached

½ small avocado, sliced

2 tbsp black beans, warmed

1 tbsp diced tomatoes

1 tbsp chopped cilantro

½ tsp red pepper flakes

Squeeze of fresh lime juice

1. Preheat the waffle iron and lightly brush it with olive oil to prevent sticking.

2. In a bowl, combine almond flour, flaxseed, baking powder, turmeric, cumin, and sea salt. Add the egg, almond milk, and olive oil, and stir until smooth.

3. Pour the batter into the waffle iron and cook for 3-4 minutes, or until golden and crispy.

4. While the waffle cooks, fry or poach the egg to your preference.

5. Place the waffle on a plate, then top with the egg, avocado slices, black beans, tomatoes, and cilantro. Squeeze fresh lime juice over everything and season with red pepper flakes for a kick.

Nom Nom your Way to not Feeling like Garbage | **Irene Fields**

Egg & Veggie Burrito

Prep Time: 10 minutes

Cook Time: 10 minutes

Servings: 1 (makes 1 large burrito

Pro Tip & Variation:

Add black beans or cooked quinoa to make it heartier.

Want more crunch? Mix in shredded cabbage or radish slices.

For a spicy twist, drizzle with hot sauce or add diced jalapeño.

2 large pasture-raised eggs

1 tbsp unsweetened almond milk

¼ tsp turmeric powder

Pinch of black pepper

Pinch of sea salt

1 tbsp extra virgin olive oil

½ cup baby spinach, chopped

¼ cup bell peppers, diced (any color)

¼ cup zucchini, diced

½ small avocado, sliced

1 tbsp fresh cilantro, chopped

1 small whole-grain or grain-free tortilla

Optional toppings: salsa, red pepper flakes, hemp seeds

1. In a mixing bowl, combine the eggs, almond milk, turmeric, black pepper, and sea salt. Beat until smooth.

2. In a nonstick pan, heat the olive oil on medium heat. Sauté bell peppers and zucchini for 2-3 minutes, until softened. Cook for an additional 30 seconds until the spinach has wilted completely.

3. Push the vegetables to one side of the pan and pour in the eggs. Allow them to sit for 10 seconds before gently stirring and cooking until just set (around 2 minutes).

4. To assemble the burrito, warm the tortilla and layer scrambled eggs and vegetables in the center. Add avocado slices and cilantro.

5. Fold the bottom up, tuck the sides, and roll tightly. Slice in half and enjoy

Nom Nom your Way to not Feeling like Garbage | Irene Fields

Mushroom & Spinach Frittata

Prep Time: 10 minutes

Cook Time: 20 minutes

Servings: 2 (makes 4 thick slices

Pro Tip & Variation:

Add smoked salmon or shredded chicken for more protein.

No oven-safe skillet?

Place in a greased baking dish before baking.

Dairy-free option? Substitute nutritional yeast for cheese flavor.

Add extra crunch? Season with toasted pumpkin seeds or walnuts.

- 4 large pasture-raised eggs
- ¼ cup unsweetened almond milk
- ½ tsp turmeric powder
- Pinch of black pepper
- Pinch of sea salt
- 1 tbsp extra virgin olive oil
- 1 cup baby spinach, chopped
- ½ cup mushrooms sliced (shiitake or cremini work great!)
- 1 small garlic clove, minced
- 2 tbsp fresh herbs (parsley, cilantro, or basil)
- Optional toppings: avocado slices, red pepper flakes, crumbled feta

1. Preheat the oven to 375°F (190°C) and prepare. Whisk together the eggs, almond milk, turmeric, black pepper, and sea salt.

2. Heat the olive oil in a oven-safe skillet over medium heat. Add the mushrooms and cook for 3-4 minutes, until tender. Cook for an additional 30 seconds until the garlic and spinach are wilted.

3. Pour the egg mixture over the vegetables and gently stir to distribute evenly. Allow it to cook on the stovetop for 2 minutes, until the edges begin to set.

4. Bake to perfection. Place the skillet in the oven for 12-15 minutes, or until the frittata is firm and golden.

5. Allow to cool for 5 minutes before serving. Cut into wedges. For extra flavor, add avocado, herbs, or crumbled feta.

Nom Nom your Way to not Feeling like Garbage | **Irene Fields**

Banana Oat Pancakes

Prep Time: 5 minutes

Cook Time: 10 minutes

Servings: 1 (makes 3 medium pancake

Pro Tip & Variation:

Add 1 tbsp ground flaxseed for more fiber.

For a crunchier texture, add chopped walnuts or pecans.

Replace eggs with a flax egg (1 tbsp flaxseed + 3 tbsp water).

Add a scoop of clean protein powder for extra protein.

- 1 ripe banana, mashed
- ½ cup rolled oats (or oat flour)
- 1 large pasture-raised egg
- ¼ cup unsweetened almond milk
- ½ tsp baking powder
- ¼ tsp turmeric powder
- Pinch of black pepper
- ½ tsp cinnamon
- 1 tsp vanilla extract
- 1 tbsp extra virgin olive oil
- Optional toppings: fresh berries, nut butter, hemp seeds, honey

1. Blend or mix. If using rolled oats, make a fine flour. In a bowl, combine the banana, egg, almond milk, turmeric, black pepper, cinnamon, and vanilla. Mix in the oat flour and baking powder until smooth.

2. Heat a non-stick skillet over medium heat and add olive oil.

3. Cook the pancakes. Add small circles of batter to the pan. Cook for 2-3 minutes until bubbles appear on the surface, then flip and cook for an additional 1-2 minutes until golden brown.

4. Stack your pancakes with fresh berries, nut butter, hemp seeds, or honey.

Nom Nom your Way to not Feeling like Garbage | **Irene Fields**

Sweet Potato Waffles

Prep Time: 10 minutes

Cook Time: 5 minutes per waffle

Servings: 1 (makes 1 large waffle or 2 small waffleS)

Pro Tips & Variations:

If you don't have a waffle iron, cook pancakes in a pan over medium heat for 2-3 minutes per side.

Want more protein? Add a scoop of collagen or plant-based protein powder

Want a crunchier texture? Toss in 1 tablespoon chopped pecans or walnuts.

Can I make it dairy-free? It already is! But the coconut yogurt on top is a nice touch.

½ cup mashed sweet potato (cooked and cooled)

1 large pasture-raised egg

¼ cup unsweetened almond milk

¼ cup almond flour

2 tbsp ground flaxseed

½ tsp baking powder

½ tsp cinnamon

¼ tsp turmeric powder

Pinch of black pepper

Pinch of sea salt

1 tbsp extra virgin olive oil

Toppings (optional):

Sliced bananas or fresh berries

Nut butter or coconut yogurt

Hemp seeds or crushed walnuts

Drizzle of honey or maple syrup

1. Preheat the waffle iron and lightly brush it with olive or coconut oil to prevent sticking.

2. In a mixing bowl, combine mashed sweet potato, egg, almond milk, cinnamon, turmeric, black pepper, and sea salt to make the batter. Mix in the almond flour, flaxseed, and baking powder until smooth.

3. Pour the batter into the waffle iron and cook for 4-5 minutes, or until golden and crisp.

4. Serve warm with your favorite toppings, such as fresh fruit, nut butter, or a drizzle of honey for added flavor!

Pumpkin Spice Pancakes

Prep Time: 5 minutes

Cook Time: 10 minutes

Servings: 1 (makes 3 medium pancakES

Pro Tip & Variation:

No eggs? Swap in a flax egg (1 tbsp flaxseed + 3 tbsp water).

For extra fluffiness, add ½ tsp apple cider vinegar to the batter.

For more protein, add a scoop of vanilla protein powder.

If you love chocolate, add some. Add cacao nibs for an extra antioxidant boost.

¼ cup pumpkin purée (not pumpkin pie filling)

1 large pasture-raised egg

¼ cup unsweetened almond milk

½ cup rolled oats (blended into oat flour)

1 tbsp ground flaxseed

½ tsp baking powder

½ tsp pumpkin spice (or mix cinnamon, nutmeg, ginger, and cloves)

¼ tsp turmeric powder

Pinch of black pepper

½ tsp vanilla extract

1 tsp maple syrup or honey

1 tbsp extra virgin olive oil

Toppings (optional):

Sliced bananas or fresh berries

Nut butter or coconut yogurt

Chopped pecans or walnuts

Extra drizzle of maple syrup

1. If using rolled oats, make a fine flour. In a bowl, combine the pumpkin, egg, almond milk, vanilla, maple syrup, and spices. Mix in the oat flour, flaxseed, and baking powder until smooth.

2. Heat a non-stick skillet over medium heat and add olive oil.

3. Add small circles of batter to the pan. Cook for 2-3 minutes until bubbles appear on the surface, then flip and cook for an additional 1-2 minutes until golden brown.

4. Stack your pancakes and top with fresh fruit, nut butter, or a sprinkle of chopped pecans for extra crunch.

Nom Nom your Way to not Feeling like Garbage | Irene Fields

Blueberry, Banana & Chia Muffins

Prep Time: 10 minutes

Cook Time: 20-22 minutes

Servings: 6 muffins

Pro Tips & Variations:

Add more protein? Add a scoop of vanilla protein powder

Make it extra fluffy? Stir in ½ tsp apple cider vinegar.

For a crunchy texture, add chopped walnuts or sunflower seeds. If you don't have almond flour, use oat flour for a nut-free option.

- 1 ripe banana, mashed
- 1 large pasture-raised egg (or flax egg: 1 tbsp flaxseed + 3 tbsp water)
- ¼ cup unsweetened almond milk
- 2 tbsp extra virgin olive oil
- 1 tsp vanilla extract
- ½ cup almond flour
- ¼ cup rolled oats
- ½ tsp baking powder
- ½ tsp cinnamon
- ¼ tsp turmeric powder
- Pinch of black pepper
- Pinch of sea salt
- ½ cup fresh or frozen blueberries
- 2 tbsp ground flaxseed
- 1 tbsp chia seeds

1. Preheat the oven to 350°F (175°C) and prepare. Line a muffin tin with 6 liners or lightly coat with olive oil.

2. In a bowl, combine the wet ingredients: mashed banana, egg, almond milk, olive oil, and vanilla.

3. In a separate bowl, combine the dry ingredients: almond flour, oats, flaxseed, chia seeds, baking powder, cinnamon, turmeric, black pepper, and sea salt.

4. Add the dry ingredients to the wet, stirring until well combined. Gently fold in the blueberries.

5. Distribute batter evenly in muffin tins. Bake for 20-22 minutes, or until a toothpick inserted into the center comes out clean.

6. Allow muffins to cool for 5 minutes before transferring to a wire rack. Enjoy. Enjoy warm or save for later

Nom Nom your Way to not Feeling like Garbage | **Irene Fields**

Breakfast Burritos with Refried Beans and Veggies

Prep Time: 10 minutes

Cook Time: 10 minutes

Servings: 1 (makes 1 large burrito)

1 small whole-grain or grain-free tortilla

2 tbsp refried black beans (use homemade or a low-sodium option)

1 large pasture-raised egg, scrambled (or ¼ cup crumbled tofu for a vegan option)

½ cup baby spinach, chopped

¼ cup bell peppers, diced (any color)

¼ cup zucchini, diced

1 tbsp red onion, finely chopped

1 small garlic clove, minced

½ tsp cumin

¼ tsp turmeric powder

Pinch of black pepper

Pinch of sea salt

1 tbsp extra virgin olive oil

Toppings (optional):

¼ small avocado, sliced

1 tbsp fresh cilantro, chopped

Squeeze of fresh lime juice

Hot sauce or salsa for extra flavor

1. To sauté vegetables, heat olive oil in a pan over medium heat. Combine red onion, bell peppers, zucchini, and garlic. Sauté for 3-4 minutes, until softened. Combine the spinach, cumin, turmeric, black pepper, and sea salt. Cook for another 30 seconds, until the spinach has wilted.

2. Scramble the eggs (or tofu) and push the vegetables to the side of the pan. If using eggs, add them and scramble for 1-2 minutes until fluffy. If using tofu, crumble it in, combine with the vegetables, and cook for 2 minutes until heated through.

Nom Nom your Way to not Feeling like Garbage | Irene Fields

3. Cook the tortilla in a dry pan for 30 seconds per side. Spread the refried beans down the middle.

4. Scrambled eggs (or tofu) and sautéed vegetables are layered on top of the beans. Combine avocado slices, cilantro, and a squeeze of lime.

5. Wrap and serve by folding the bottom up, tucking in the sides, and rolling tightly. Slice in half and serve warm!

Pro Tip & Variation: Add more protein with hemp seeds or nutritional yeast.

No tortilla? Wrap everything in a large collard green for a low-carb option.

To make it spicier, add diced jalapeños or a drizzle of hot sauce.

For extra crunch, add shredded cabbage or radish slices.

Avocado Toast with Sriracha

Prep Time: 5 minutes

Cook Time: 0 minutes

Servings: 1 (makes 1 slice of toast

Pro Tip & Variation:

Add more protein by poaching or frying an egg on top.

Additional crunch? Season with toasted pumpkin seeds or crushed nuts.

For a different heat, substitute chili flakes, harissa, or hot honey. For a Mexican twist, add fresh pico de gallo or crumbled cotija cheese.

1 slice whole-grain, sourdough, or gluten-free bread (toasted)

½ ripe avocado, mashed

½ tsp fresh lemon or lime juice

¼ tsp turmeric powder

Pinch of black pepper

Pinch of sea salt

1 tsp sriracha or More

Optional toppings:

1 tbsp hemp seeds

½ tsp red pepper flakes

1 tbsp chopped fresh cilantro

1 soft-boiled or fried egg

1. Toast the bread until golden and crispy.

2. In a small bowl, combine the avocado, lemon/lime juice, turmeric, black pepper, and sea salt.

3. Assemble the toast and spread the mashed avocado evenly.

4. Drizzle sriracha on top and add desired toppings.

Scrambled Egg with Dill, Avocado, and Feta on Sourdough

Prep Time: 5 minutes

Cook Time: 5 minutes

Servings: 1 (makes 1 loaded slice of toast

Pro Tip & Variation:

For more protein, add smoked salmon or hemp seeds.

If feta is not available, substitute goat cheese or a dairy-free alternative.

For a spicier option, drizzle with hot honey or sriracha.

Gluten-free? Replace sourdough with a grain-free or gluten-free bread.

1 slice sourdough bread (toasted)

2 large pasture-raised eggs

1 tbsp unsweetened almond milk

½ tbsp extra virgin olive oil (or grass-fed butter)

Pinch of sea salt

Pinch of black pepper

½ ripe avocado, sliced or mashed

1 tbsp feta cheese, crumbled

1 tsp fresh dill, chopped (or ¼ tsp dried)

Optional toppings: red pepper flakes, hemp seeds, extra drizzle of olive oil

1. Toast the sourdough bread until golden and crispy.

2. In a bowl, combine the eggs, almond milk, salt, and pepper. Heat the olive oil in a pan over medium-low heat, then add the eggs. Stir slowly with a spatula until just set but still creamy, about 2-3 minutes.

3. To assemble the toast, spread mashed avocado on the sourdough. Pile the softly scrambled eggs on top.

4. Sprinkle crumbled feta and fresh dill over the eggs. Add a pinch of red pepper flakes or hemp seeds if desired.

Nom Nom your Way to not Feeling like Garbage | Irene Fields

Chia Pudding Topped with Flax, Hemp, and Goji Berries

Prep Time: 5 minutes

Chill Time: 2 hours (or overnight)

Servings: 1 (makes 1 cup of pudding

Pro Tip & Variation:

For a creamier texture, blend the pudding.

Want more protein? Add a scoop of plant-based protein powder.

If you don't have goji berries, use fresh berries or cacao nibs instead.

Want to make it chocolatey? Add 1 tsp cacao powder for a richer flavor.

3 tbsp chia seeds

¾ cup unsweetened almond milk (or coconut milk for extra creaminess)

½ tsp vanilla extract

½ tsp cinnamon

1 tsp maple syrup or honey

Toppings:

1 tbsp ground flaxseed

1 tbsp hemp seeds

1 tbsp goji berries

1. In a jar or bowl, combine the chia seeds, almond milk, vanilla, cinnamon, and maple syrup. Allow it to sit for 5 minutes before stirring again to avoid clumping.

2. Cover and chill for at least 2 hours (or overnight). The chia seeds will absorb the liquid and thicken, resulting in a pudding-like consistency.

3. To serve, top with flaxseed, hemp seeds, and goji berries.

Salad and Sides

Nom Nom your Way to not Feeling like Garbage | **Irene Fields**

Kale and Quinoa Salad

Prep Time: 15 minutes

Cook Time: 15 minutes

Servings: 2 (about 2 ½ cups per serving

Pro Tip & Variation:

Add more protein? Try chickpeas or grilled salmon.

For a meal, pair it with avocado and a hard-boiled egg.

For extra crunch, add pumpkin seeds or crispy roasted chickpeas.

Consider using wild rice or farro instead of quinoa.

For the Salad:

3 cups kale, destemmed and finely chopped

½ cup quinoa, uncooked (or 1 ½ cups cooked)

½ cup cherry tomatoes, halved

¼ cup red onion, finely diced

¼ cup cucumber, diced

2 tbsp hemp seeds

¼ cup toasted almonds or walnuts

For the Lemon-Tahini Dressing:

3 tbsp tahini

2 tbsp fresh lemon juice

1 tbsp extra virgin olive oil

1 tsp maple syrup or honey

1 small garlic clove, minced

¼ tsp turmeric powder

2-3 tbsp water, to thin as needed

Pinch of sea salt & black pepper

1. Rinse quinoa with cold water and cook in 1 cup water over medium heat until fluffy (approximately 12-15 minutes). Allow it to cool.

2. In a large bowl, combine chopped kale, olive oil, and salt. Massage the leaves with your hands for 1-2 minutes, until they soften and darken. This makes it more tender and easier to digest!

3. Combine all ingredients until smooth. Add more water as needed to achieve a creamy, pourable consistency.

4. Combine the massaged kale with cooked quinoa, cherry tomatoes, red onion, cucumber, hemp seeds, and nuts. Drizzle with dressing and mix thoroughly.

5. Allow 5 minutes for flavors to meld before digging in!

Nom Nom your Way to not Feeling like Garbage | **Irene Fields**

Turmeric Chickpea Salad

Prep Time: 10 minutes

Cook Time: 0 minutes (unless using dried chickpeas)

Servings: 2 (about 2 cups per serving

Pro Tip & Variation:

Make it a meal? Add grilled chicken, salmon, or boiled egg.

For extra crunch, add toasted almonds or chickpeas.

For a spicy kick, add cayenne or red pepper flakes.

Meal prep tip: Keeps well in the fridge for up to 3 days—flavors improve overnight!

For the Salad:

1 ½ cups cooked chickpeas (or 1 can, drained & rinsed)

½ cup cucumber, diced

½ cup red bell pepper, diced

¼ cup red onion, finely chopped

¼ cup fresh parsley or cilantro, chopped

2 tbsp pumpkin seeds or sunflower seeds

2 tbsp crumbled feta or diced avocado

For the Turmeric Dressing:

2 tbsp extra virgin olive oil

1 tbsp fresh lemon juice

½ tsp turmeric powder

½ tsp ground cumin

½ tsp maple syrup or honey

¼ tsp black pepper

¼ tsp sea salt

1. In a small bowl, combine olive oil, lemon juice, turmeric, cumin, maple syrup (if using), black pepper, and salt. Whisk until smooth.

2. In a large bowl, combine chickpeas, cucumber, bell pepper, red onion, fresh herbs, and seeds. Toss the salad.

3. Pour the turmeric dressing over the salad and toss to coat.

4. Allow the salad to marinate for 5-10 minutes to combine the flavors.

5. Eat as is, or top with greens, quinoa, or a whole-grain wrap.

Nom Nom your Way to not Feeling like Garbage | **Irene Fields**

Arugula and Beet Salad

Prep Time: 10 minutes

Cook Time: 0 minutes (if using pre-cooked beets) / 30-40 minutes (if roasting fresh beets)

Servings: 2 (about 2 cups per serving)

Pro Tip & Variation:

Make it a meal? Add grilled chicken, salmon, or boiled egg.

For extra crunch, add toasted almonds or chickpeas.

For a spicy kick, add cayenne or red pepper flakes.

Meal prep tip: Keeps well in the fridge for up to 3 days—flavors improve overnight!

For the Salad:

3 cups arugula, loosely packed

1 medium beet, roasted & thinly sliced (or ½ cup pre-cooked beets, sliced)

¼ cup walnuts, toasted & chopped

¼ cup goat cheese or feta, crumbled

¼ cup pomegranate seeds

2 tbsp hemp seeds

For the Citrus Dressing:

3 tbsp extra virgin olive oil

1 tbsp fresh lemon juice

1 tbsp fresh orange juice

1 tsp honey or maple syrup

½ tsp Dijon mustard

¼ tsp sea salt

¼ tsp black pepper

1. In a small bowl, combine olive oil, lemon juice, turmeric, cumin, maple syrup (if using), black pepper, and salt. Whisk until smooth.

2. In a large bowl, combine chickpeas, cucumber, bell pepper, red onion, fresh herbs, and seeds. Toss the salad.

3. Pour the turmeric dressing over the salad and toss to coat.

4. Allow the salad to marinate for 5-10 minutes to combine the flavors.

5. Eat as is, or top with greens, quinoa, or a whole-grain wrap.

Nom Nom your Way to not Feeling like Garbage | **Irene Fields**

Mediterranean Lentil Salad

Prep Time: 10 minutes

Cook Time: 20 minutes (for lentils)

Servings: 2 (about 2 cups per serving)

For the Salad:

1 cup cooked green or brown lentils (or ½ cup dry lentils, cooked)

½ cup cucumber, diced

½ cup cherry tomatoes, halved

¼ cup red onion, finely diced

¼ cup bell pepper (red or yellow), diced

¼ cup kalamata olives, sliced

¼ cup fresh parsley, chopped

2 tbsp feta cheese

2 tbsp toasted pine nuts or walnuts

For the Lemon-Olive Oil Dressing:

3 tbsp extra virgin olive oil

2 tbsp fresh lemon juice

1 small garlic clove, minced

½ tsp ground cumin

½ tsp dried oregano

¼ tsp sea salt

¼ tsp black pepper

1. In a small bowl, combine olive oil, lemon juice, turmeric, cumin, maple syrup (if using), black pepper, and salt. Whisk until smooth.

2. In a large bowl, combine chickpeas, cucumber, bell pepper, red onion, fresh herbs, and seeds. Toss the salad.

3. Pour the turmeric dressing over the salad and toss to coat.

4. Allow the salad to marinate for 5-10 minutes to combine the flavors.

5. Eat as is, or top with greens, quinoa, or a whole-grain wrap.

Nom Nom your Way to not Feeling like Garbage | **Irene Fields**

Cauliflower Rice Salad

Prep Time: 10 minutes

Cook Time: 5 minutes

Servings: 2 (about 2 cups per serving

Pro Tip & Variation:

Make it a meal? Add grilled shrimp, chickpeas, or avocado.

To add crunch, toss in pumpkin seeds or roasted chickpeas. For a spicy kick, add a pinch of cayenne or red pepper flakes. Meal prep tip: Keeps fresh in the fridge for up to 3 days—just keep the dressing separate!

For the Salad:

2 cups cauliflower rice (store-bought or homemade)

½ cup cherry tomatoes, halved

½ cup cucumber, diced

¼ cup red bell pepper, diced

¼ cup red onion, finely chopped

¼ cup fresh parsley, chopped

2 tbsp toasted almonds or walnuts

2 tbsp hemp seeds

For the Lemon-Turmeric Dressing:

3 tbsp extra virgin olive oil

2 tbsp fresh lemon juice

½ tsp turmeric powder

½ tsp ground cumin

½ tsp honey or maple syrup

¼ tsp sea salt

¼ tsp black pepper

1. Optional: lightly cook cauliflower rice. Skip this step if you prefer it raw.

For a softer texture, sauté the cauliflower rice in 1 tsp olive oil over medium heat for 2-3 minutes. Allow it to cool.

2. In a small bowl, combine the olive oil, lemon juice, turmeric, cumin, honey, salt, and black pepper.

3. In a large bowl, combine the cauliflower rice, cherry tomatoes, cucumber, bell pepper, red onion, and parsley.

4. Pour the lemon-turmeric dressing over the salad and toss thoroughly. Allow to sit for 5 minutes so the flavors can meld.

5. Sprinkle it with toasted nuts and hemp seeds before serving.

Nom Nom your Way to not Feeling like Garbage | Irene Fields

Tofu and Veggie Wrap

Prep Time: 10 minutes

Cook Time: 10 minutes

Servings: 2 wraps (1 wrap per serving)

For the Wraps:

6 oz extra-firm tofu, pressed & sliced into strips

½ tsp turmeric powder

½ tsp cumin powder

1 tbsp extra virgin olive oil

½ cup red bell pepper, julienned

½ cup cucumber, julienned

½ cup shredded carrots

¼ cup red cabbage, shredded

¼ cup avocado, sliced

¼ cup microgreens or baby spinach

2 whole grain or gluten-free wraps

For the Tahini-Turmeric Dressing:

2 tbsp tahini

1 tbsp fresh lemon juice

½ tsp turmeric powder

½ tsp maple syrup or honey

1 small garlic clove, minced

2-3 tbsp water (to thin)

Pinch of sea salt & black pepper

1. To cook the tofu, heat 1 tablespoon of olive oil in a pan over medium heat.

- Season the tofu strips with turmeric, cumin, salt, and pepper.

- Cook for 3-4 minutes on each side until golden and crispy.

2. Prepare the dressing.

- Whisk together the tahini, lemon juice, turmeric, maple syrup, garlic, salt, and black pepper.

- Add water one tablespoon at a time until smooth and pourable.

Nom Nom your Way to not Feeling like Garbage | **Irene Fields**

3. Assemble the wraps by laying them flat and spreading 1 tbsp of dressing in the center.

- Arrange the spinach, bell pepper, cucumber, carrots, cabbage, tofu, and avocado.

4. Wrap it up! - Fold sides in and roll tightly from bottom up.

- Cut in half and enjoy

Pro Tips & Variations:

Go grain-free? Replace the wrap with collard greens or lettuce cups.

For extra crunch, add toasted pumpkin or hemp seeds.

For a spicy kick, add cayenne or chili flakes to the tofu.

Meal prep tip: Keep the dressing separate and assemble fresh for the best texture!

Garlic Green Beans

Prep Time: 5 minutes

Cook Time: 10 minutes

Servings: 2 (about 1 cup per serving)

Pro Tip & Variation:

Add pumpkin or hemp seeds for extra crunch.

If you like it spicy, add more red pepper flakes or cayenne.

For a complete meal, pair with grilled salmon or quinoa.

Meal prep tip: Keeps fresh in the fridge for up to 3 days; reheat lightly in a pan for the best texture!

2 cups fresh green beans, trimmed

1 tbsp extra virgin olive oil

2 cloves garlic, minced

¼ tsp turmeric powder

¼ tsp red pepper flakes

¼ tsp sea salt

¼ tsp black pepper

1 tsp fresh lemon juice

1 tbsp toasted almonds or sesame seeds

1. Optional but recommended: blanch the green beans.

- Bring salted water to a boil.

- Add green beans and cook for 2 minutes before draining and transferring to an ice bath.

2. To sauté garlic, heat olive oil in a large pan over medium heat.

- Add the garlic and cook for 30 seconds, stirring constantly, until fragrant.

3. Cook the green beans.

- Place the blanched green beans in the pan.

- Season with turmeric, red pepper flakes, salt, and black pepper.

- Sauté for 4-5 minutes, tossing frequently, until tender and crisp.

4. Finish with lemon and toppings. Remove from heat and drizzle with fresh lemon juice.

- Top with toasted almonds or sesame seeds, if desired.

Nom Nom your Way to not Feeling like Garbage | **Irene Fields**

Sweet Potato Fries

Prep Time: 10 minutes

Cook Time: 25-30 minutes

Servings: 2 (about 1 cup per serving)

Pro Tips & Variations:

Want more crispiness? Soak the fries in cold water for 30 minutes before baking, and then thoroughly dry.

To make it spicy, add a pinch of cayenne or red pepper flakes.

No oven? Air-fry at 375°F (190°C) for 15-18 minutes, shaking halfway.

Meal preparation tip: Keep leftovers in an airtight container for up to **three days**. Reheat in the oven for optimal texture.

For the Fries:

2 medium sweet potatoes, cut into ¼-inch fries

1 tbsp extra virgin olive oil

½ tsp turmeric powder

½ tsp paprika

½ tsp garlic powder

¼ tsp cinnamon

¼ tsp sea salt

¼ tsp black pepper

For the Dipping Sauce (Optional):

¼ cup Greek yogurt or tahini

1 tbsp fresh lemon juice

½ tsp honey or maple syrup

¼ tsp cumin

Pinch of sea salt

1. Preheat the oven to 425°F (220°C). Line a baking sheet with parchment paper for easy cleanup.

2. Cut and season sweet potatoes into uniform ¼-inch fries (for even cooking).

- Toss with olive oil, turmeric, paprika, garlic powder, cinnamon (optional), salt, and pepper.

3. Bake until crispy perfection.

- Arrange the fries in a single layer on the baking sheet (do not overcrowd).

- Bake for 25-30 minutes, flipping halfway through, until golden and crispy around the edges.

4. Make the dipping sauce (optional).

- Mix together the Greek yogurt (or tahini), lemon juice, honey, cumin, and salt.

Allow the fries to cool for a minute before digging in

Nom Nom your Way to not Feeling like Garbage | **Irene Fields**

Black Bean & Sweet Potato Patties

Prep Time: 10 minutes

Cook Time: 15 minutes

Servings: 4 patties (1 patty per serving

Pro Tip & Variation:

Want it spicy? Add a pinch of cayenne or chili flakes.

For extra crunch, lightly coat patties with crushed walnuts or seeds before cooking.

What is the oven method? Bake at 375°F (190°C) for 20 minutes, flipping halfway through.

Meal prep tip: Refrigerate for up to 4 days, or freeze for later

- 1 cup mashed sweet potato (about 1 medium sweet potato, roasted & mashed)
- 1 cup black beans, drained & mashed
- ¼ cup oats or almond flour (for binding)
- ¼ cup red onion, finely diced
- 1 clove garlic, minced
- ½ tsp turmeric powder
- ½ tsp ground cumin
- ½ tsp paprika
- ¼ tsp sea salt
- ¼ tsp black pepper
- 1 tbsp flaxseed meal + 2 tbsp water (egg substitute for binding)
- 1 tbsp extra virgin olive oil

1. Combine 1 tbsp flaxseed meal with 2 tbsp water and set aside for 5 minutes to thicken.

2. In a large bowl, mash and mix the black beans until mostly smooth.

- Combine mashed sweet potatoes, oats/almond flour, onion, garlic, spices, and flax egg.

- Mix until a thick dough is formed. If the mixture is too wet, add extra oats or flour.

3. Divide the mixture into four equal portions and shape into patties.

4. Heat 1 tbsp olive oil in a pan on medium heat.

- Cook the patties for 3-4 minutes per side, until golden and firm.

5. Use it as a burger patty, bowl, or wrap in lettuce or whole-grain wrap

Nom Nom your Way to not Feeling like Garbage | Irene Fields

Vegetarian and Vegan

Nom Nom your Way to not Feeling like Garbage | **Irene Fields**

Caprese-Stuffed Portobello Mushrooms

Prep Time: 10 minutes

Cook Time: 15 minutes

Servings: 2 (Each serving = 1 large stuffed mushroom cap)

Pro Tips & Variations:

Add protein? Try shredded rotisserie chicken or grilled tofu.

Want more greens? Add arugula or baby spinach before baking.

Make it heartier? Serve with quinoa or zucchini noodles.

No dairy-free cheese?. Avocado slices make a creamy alternative.

2 large Portobello mushroom caps, stems removed

1 tbsp extra virgin olive oil

½ tsp balsamic vinegar

¼ tsp sea salt

¼ tsp black pepper

½ cup cherry tomatoes, halved

¼ cup dairy-free mozzarella (or crumbled almond feta)

2 tbsp fresh basil, chopped

2 tbsp pesto (recipe below)

1 tbsp pine nuts

Quick Anti-Inflammatory Pesto:

½ cup fresh basil

1 tbsp extra virgin olive oil

1 tbsp walnuts (or hemp seeds for omega-3 boost)

1 tsp lemon juice

1 small garlic clove

Pinch of sea salt & black pepper

Blend until smooth and set aside.

1. Preheat and prepare your oven to 400°F (200°C). Brush olive oil and balsamic vinegar onto both sides of the mushroom caps, then season with salt and pepper.

2. Place the mushrooms on a baking sheet, gill side up, and roast for 10 minutes, or until tender but still holding shape.

3. Fill each mushroom cap with cherry tomatoes, dairy-free mozzarella, and chopped basil.

4. Return to the oven for 5 minutes to soften the cheese and warm everything up.

5. Add a spoonful of homemade pesto and a sprinkle of pine nuts for texture. Serve

Nom Nom your Way to not Feeling like Garbage | **Irene Fields**

Sweet Potato-Black Bean Tacos

Prep Time: 10 minutes

Cook Time: 25 minutes

Servings: 2 (Makes 4 tacos)

Pro Tip & Variation:

Add shredded purple cabbage or pickled onions for extra crunch.

For more protein, add grilled tofu or shredded rotisserie chicken.

For a spicy twist, drizzle with hot sauce or add jalapeño slices.

For a grain-free option, substitute lettuce cups for tortillas.

1 medium sweet potato, peeled & diced (about 1 ½ cups)

1 tbsp extra virgin olive oil

½ tsp ground cumin

½ tsp smoked paprika

¼ tsp turmeric powder

¼ tsp sea salt

1 cup black beans, drained & rinsed

¼ cup red onion, finely diced

½ lime, juiced

4 small corn tortillas (or grain-free tortillas)

Toppings (pick your faves):

½ avocado, sliced

Fresh cilantro, chopped

2 tbsp dairy-free yogurt or cashew crema

2 tbsp crumbled almond feta

1 tbsp pumpkin seeds

1. To roast sweet potatoes, preheat the oven to 400°F (200°C). Mix the diced sweet potatoes with olive oil, cumin, smoked paprika, turmeric, and sea salt. Spread onto a baking sheet and roast for 20-25 minutes, flipping halfway through, until golden and tender.

2. In a small pan over medium heat, warm the black beans, red onion, and lime juice for 2-3 minutes, or until heated through.

3. To toast the tortillas, heat a dry skillet over medium heat for 30 seconds per side, until soft and slightly charred.

4. To assemble the tacos, fill each tortilla with roasted sweet potatoes and black beans. Add your favorite toppings, such as avocado, cilantro, dairy-free yogurt, or pumpkin seeds for crunch.

5. Squeeze extra lime juice on top and devour

Nom Nom your Way to not Feeling like Garbage | Irene Fields

Stir-fried tofu and vegetables

Prep Time: 10 minutes

Cook Time: 10 minutes

Servings: 2 (Makes about 3 cups of stir-fry)

Pro Tip & Variation:

Add water chestnuts or snap peas for extra crunch.

For a spicy kick, drizzle with Sriracha or sprinkle with red pepper flakes.

For extra protein, add cooked quinoa or chickpeas.

If tofu is unavailable, substitute tempeh or mushrooms.

For the tofu:

½ block (7 oz) extra-firm tofu, pressed & cubed

1 tbsp extra virgin olive oil or avocado oil

½ tsp turmeric powder

¼ tsp sea salt

¼ tsp black pepper

For the stir-fry:

1 tbsp sesame oil (or more olive oil)

1 cup broccoli florets

½ cup red bell pepper, sliced

½ cup zucchini, sliced

½ cup carrots, julienned

1-inch piece ginger, grated

2 cloves garlic, minced

2 tbsp coconut aminos (or low-sodium tamari)

1 tbsp lime juice

1 tsp sesame seeds

Optional toppings: sliced green onions, crushed peanuts, or hemp seeds

1. In a large pan, heat olive oil on medium-high heat. Mix in the cubed tofu, turmeric, sea salt, and black pepper. Cook for 4-5 minutes, flipping occasionally, or until golden and crispy. Remove from the pan and set aside.

2. Sauté the vegetables in the same pan with sesame oil. Combine the broccoli, bell pepper, zucchini, and carrots. Stir-fry for 3-4 minutes, until slightly tender but crisp.

3. Combine grated ginger and minced garlic. Stir continuously for 30 seconds, until fragrant.

4. Mix in coconut aminos and lime juice. Stir everything together and cook for one more minute.

5. Return the crispy tofu to the pan, toss, and cook for an additional minute to absorb the flavors.

6. Plate it, top with sesame seeds or your favorite toppings, and dig in!

Nom Nom your Way to not Feeling like Garbage | **Irene Fields**

Grilled vegetable and pesto pasta

Prep Time: 10 minutes

Cook Time: 15 minutes

Servings: 2 (Makes about 3 cups of pasta)

Pro Tip & Variation:

Add grilled tofu, chickpeas, or salmon for extra protein.

No grill? Roast the vegetables at 400°F (200°C) for 15 minutes. Are they nut-free? Swap walnuts with sunflower seeds or more olive oil.

Want a spicy kick? Add some red pepper flakes or a drizzle of chili oil.

For the pasta:

4 oz chickpea or quinoa pasta

1 small zucchini, sliced into rounds

½ red bell pepper, sliced

½ red onion, sliced

1 small eggplant, sliced into rounds

1 tbsp extra virgin olive oil

¼ tsp sea salt

¼ tsp black pepper

For the anti-inflammatory pesto:

½ cup fresh basil

¼ cup walnuts (or hemp seeds for an omega-3 boost)

1 tbsp extra virgin olive oil

1 tbsp lemon juice

1 small garlic clove

Pinch of sea salt & black pepper

1. Cook pasta: Bring salted water to a boil, then cook according to package instructions. Drain and set aside.

2. Preheat a grill pan or outdoor grill to medium-high heat. Mix the zucchini, bell pepper, red onion, and eggplant with olive oil, salt, and black pepper. Grill for 2-3 minutes per side, until lightly charred and tender. Remove from heat.

3. In a small food processor or blender, combine the basil, walnuts, olive oil, lemon juice, garlic, salt, and black pepper. Blend until smooth, using a splash of water as needed.

4. Toss cooked pasta with pesto in a large bowl until evenly coated. Add the grilled vegetables and gently combine.

5. Plate it and garnish with additional basil or hemp seeds for extra nutrients.

Thai red curry with tofu over rice

Prep Time: 10 minutes

Cook Time: 20 minutes

Servings: 2 (Makes about 3 cups of curry, served over 2 cups rice)

For the tofu:

½ block (7 oz) extra-firm tofu, pressed & cubed

1 tbsp coconut oil or avocado oil

½ tsp turmeric powder

¼ tsp sea salt

¼ tsp black pepper

For the curry:

1 tbsp coconut oil

½ red onion, sliced

1-inch piece ginger, grated

2 cloves garlic, minced

2 tbsp Thai red curry paste (look for one without additives!)

1 cup full-fat coconut milk

½ cup vegetable broth (or water)

1 small red bell pepper, sliced

½ cup broccoli florets

½ cup carrots, julienned

1 tsp lime juice

1 tsp coconut aminos (or low-sodium tamari)

For serving:

1 cup cooked jasmine or brown rice per serving

Toppings (optional): fresh cilantro, lime wedges, sliced chili, toasted sesame seeds

1. Heat 1 tbsp coconut oil in a pan over medium-high heat. Toss the tofu cubes with turmeric, sea salt, and black pepper. Cook for 4-5 minutes, flipping occasionally, or until golden and crispy. Remove from the pan and set aside.

2. In the same pan, heat an additional tbsp coconut oil over medium heat. Add the red onion and cook for 2 minutes until softened. Cook for 30 seconds, stirring in the garlic, ginger, and Thai red curry paste until fragrant.

3. Pour in the coconut milk and vegetable broth, stirring thoroughly to combine. Bring to a simmer.

Nom Nom your Way to not Feeling like Garbage | **Irene Fields**

4. Toss in the veggies: bell pepper, broccoli, and carrots. Simmer for 5-7 minutes, until the vegetables are tender but vibrant.

5. Add lime juice and coconut aminos for extra flavor. Return the crispy tofu to the pan and let it soak up the flavors for another minute.

6. Serve and enjoy the curry with warm jasmine or brown rice. Garnish with fresh cilantro, lime, and optional toppings.

Pro Tips & Variations:

Add extra protein? Add chickpeas or edamame.

Spice it up? Stir in a chopped Thai chili or a dash of Sriracha.

For a nutty twist, add almond or cashew butter.

If tofu is not available, substitute tempeh, mushrooms, or cauliflower.

Garlic and chili veggie stir fry Noodles

Prep Time: 10 minutes

Cook Time: 10 minutes

Servings: 2 (Makes about 3 cups of stir-fry noodles)

Pro Tip & Variation:

Add more protein with tofu, tempeh, or chickpeas.

To add crunch, add cashews or almonds. For a spicy twist, drizzle with sriracha or chili oil. If you don't have rice noodles, use soba or whole wheat noodles instead.

2 cloves garlic, minced

1-inch piece ginger, grated

1 small red chili, finely chopped (adjust for spice level)

½ tsp turmeric powder

For the stir-fry veggies:

½ cup red bell pepper, sliced

½ cup broccoli florets

½ cup carrots, julienned

½ cup snap peas (or green beans)

1 tbsp coconut aminos (or low-sodium tamari)

1 tsp rice vinegar

½ tsp maple syrup

For topping:

1 tbsp sesame seeds

1 tbsp green onions, sliced

Lime wedges for serving

For the noodles:

4 oz rice noodles (or zucchini noodles for a low-carb option)

1 tbsp sesame oil or avocado oil

1. Cook the rice noodles per package instructions. Drain, rinse in cold water, and set aside.

2. Heat the sesame oil in a large pan or wok over medium heat. Combine garlic, ginger, chili, and turmeric. Stir for 30 seconds, until fragrant.

3. Cook the veggies, including bell pepper, broccoli, carrots, and snap peas. Stir-fry for 3-4 minutes to keep the vegetables crisp and vibrant.

4. Combine cooked noodles, coconut aminos, rice vinegar, and maple syrup to make the sauce. Stir thoroughly, ensuring that everything is coated. Cook for an additional 1-2 minutes.

5. Plate the noodles and garnish with sesame seeds and green onions. Serve with lime wedges for a refreshing citrus kick

Nom Nom your Way to not Feeling like Garbage | Irene Fields

Halloumi peanut curry

Prep Time: 10 minutes

Cook Time: 20 minutes

Servings: 2 (Makes about 3 cups of curry, served over 2 cups of rice)

For the halloumi:

4 oz halloumi, cut into cubes

1 tsp olive oil

For the curry:

1 tbsp coconut oil or avocado oil

½ red onion, sliced

2 cloves garlic, minced

1-inch piece ginger, grated

½ small red chili, finely chopped

½ tsp turmeric powder

1 tsp ground cumin

1 tsp ground coriander

2 tbsp natural peanut butter (unsweetened)

½ cup full-fat coconut milk

½ cup vegetable broth

1 small red bell pepper, sliced

½ cup zucchini, sliced

½ cup cherry tomatoes, halved

1 tsp lime juice

1 tsp coconut aminos (or low-sodium tamari)

For serving:

1 cup cooked jasmine or brown rice per serving

Toppings (optional): chopped peanuts, fresh cilantro, lime wedges, or chili flakes

1. Heat 1 tsp olive oil in a pan over medium-high heat. Add the halloumi cubes and sear for 2-3 minutes per side, until golden. Remove and set aside.

2. In the same pan, warm 1 tbsp coconut oil over medium heat. Add the red onion and cook for 2 minutes, until soft. Stir in the garlic, ginger, and chili. Cook for 30 seconds, until fragrant.

3. Add turmeric, cumin, and coriander, stirring for 30 seconds to toast the spices.

4. Mix in the peanut butter, coconut milk, and vegetable broth until smooth. Bring to a gentle simmer.

Nom Nom your Way to not Feeling like Garbage | **Irene Fields**

5. Add veggies, including bell pepper, zucchini, and cherry tomatoes. Simmer 5-7 minutes, until tender but not mushy.

6. Add lime juice and coconut aminos for a flavorful finish. Return the crispy halloumi to the pan and let it absorb the flavors for one minute.

7. Serve and enjoy with warm jasmine or brown rice. Garnish with chopped peanuts, fresh cilantro, and a squeeze of lime.

Pro Tips & Variations:

Add chickpeas or tofu for extra protein.

Add more chili or sriracha for a spicy kick.

For a nut-free option, replace peanut butter with tahini or sunflower seed butter

Extra creamy? Stir in 1 tablespoon cashew cream.

Chickpea Mayo

Prep Time: 5 minutes

Servings: About 1 cup

Pro Tip & Variation:

For extra creaminess, add 1 tbsp tahini or cashew cream.

For a spicy kick, add a pinch of cayenne or smoked paprika.

For a milder flavor, replace olive oil with avocado oil.

Add a zesty twist. Add a little grated lemon zest.

1 cup cooked chickpeas (or canned, drained & rinsed)

2 tbsp extra virgin olive oil

1 tbsp lemon juice

1 tsp apple cider vinegar

1 tsp Dijon mustard

½ tsp turmeric powder

½ tsp garlic powder

¼ tsp sea salt

¼ tsp black pepper

2–3 tbsp water

1. Blend all ingredients together in a food processor or blender. Blend until smooth and creamy.

2. If too thick, add water 1 tbsp at a time to achieve desired texture.

3. For balance, adjust the amount of salt, lemon, or mustard.

4. Transfer to a jar and keep refrigerated for up to 5 days.

Nom Nom your Way to not Feeling like Garbage | **Irene Fields**

Plant based vegetable frittata

Prep Time: 10 minutes

Cook Time: 20 minutes

Servings: 2 (Makes about 4 slices)

Pro Tip & Variation:

For more protein, add crumbled tofu or hemp seeds.

Want more umami? Add sun-dried tomatoes or mushrooms.

No oven? Cook on the stovetop in a covered pan over low heat for 10-12 minutes until set.

Want a spicy kick? Add some red pepper flakes or a dash of hot sauce.

For the batter:

¾ cup chickpea flour

½ cup unsweetened plant milk (almond, oat, or soy)

¼ cup water

1 tbsp nutritional yeast

½ tsp turmeric powder

½ tsp garlic powder

½ tsp onion powder

½ tsp baking powde

¼ tsp black salt (Kala Namak) (gives an eggy taste, optional)

¼ tsp black pepper

For the vegetables:

½ cup red bell pepper, diced

½ cup zucchini, diced

½ cup spinach, chopped

¼ cup red onion, diced

1 tbsp extra virgin olive oil

1. Preheat oven to 375°F (190°C) and lightly grease a small oven-safe skillet or baking dish.

2. Sauté vegetables with olive oil in a pan over medium heat. Combine red onion, bell pepper, and zucchini. Sauté for 3-4 minutes, until slightly softened. Add the spinach and cook for another minute until wilted. Remove from heat.

3. In a mixing bowl, combine chickpea flour, plant milk, water, nutritional yeast, turmeric, garlic powder, onion powder, baking powder, black salt (if using), and black pepper. Whisk until smooth. The batter should be pourable but not too runny—add more water as needed.

4. Stir the sautéed vegetables into the batter. Pour the mixture into a greased skillet or baking dish.

5. Bake in the oven for 18-20 minutes, or until firm and slightly golden on top. Allow it to rest for 5 minutes before slicing.

6. Cut into slices and serve warm. Delicious on its own or with avocado, salsa, or a side salad

Nom Nom your Way to not Feeling like Garbage | Irene Fields

Nom Nom your Way to not Feeling like Garbage | **Irene Fields**

Garlic and chili veggie stir fry Noodles

Prep Time: 10 minutes

Cook Time: 10 minutes

Servings: 2 (Makes about 3 cups of stir-fry noodles)

Pro Tip & Variation:

Add tofu, tempeh, or chickpeas for extra protein.

To add crunch, add cashews or almonds. For a spicy kick, drizzle with sriracha or chili oil. If you don't have rice noodles, use zucchini or whole wheat noodles instead.

For the noodles:

4 oz rice noodles (or soba noodles for extra protein)

1 tbsp sesame oil (or avocado oil)

2 cloves garlic, minced

1-inch piece ginger, grated

1 small red chili, finely chopped

½ tsp turmeric powder

For the stir-fry veggies:

½ cup red bell pepper, sliced

½ cup broccoli florets

½ cup carrots, julienned

½ cup snap peas or bok choy

1 tbsp coconut aminos (or low-sodium tamari)

1 tsp rice vinegar

½ tsp maple syrup

For topping:

1 tbsp sesame seeds

1 tbsp green onions, sliced

Lime wedges for serving

1. Cook the rice noodles per package instructions. Drain, rinse in cold water, and set aside.

2. Heat the sesame oil in a large pan or wok over medium heat. Combine garlic, ginger, chili, and turmeric. Stir for 30 seconds, until fragrant.

3. Cook the veggies, including bell pepper, broccoli, carrots, and snap peas. Stir-fry for 3-4 minutes to keep the vegetables crisp and vibrant.

4. Combine cooked noodles, coconut aminos, rice vinegar, and maple syrup to make the sauce. Stir thoroughly, ensuring that everything is coated. Cook for an additional 1-2 minutes.

5. Plate the noodles and garnish with sesame seeds and green onions. Serve with lime wedges for a refreshing citrus kick

Fish and Beef

Nom Nom your Way to not Feeling like Garbage | **Irene Fields**

Poached Salmon with Herbs

Prep Time: 5 minutes

Cook Time: 10 minutes

Servings: 2 (1 fillet per person, about 6 oz each)

Pro Tips & Variations:

Want a richer broth? Swap water for coconut milk for a creamy, anti-inflammatory twist.

Extra flavor boost? Add a splash of apple cider vinegar for tang and gut health benefits.

Pair with? Serve with steamed broccoli, quinoa, or a light cucumber-dill salad.

Optional: add a pinch of cayenne or red pepper flakes for heat.

2 wild-caught salmon fillets (about 6 oz each)

2 cups filtered water (or low-sodium vegetable broth)

½ lemon, sliced

2 sprigs fresh thyme (or dill)

1 garlic clove, smashed

1-inch piece ginger, sliced

½ tsp turmeric powder (or 1 tsp freshly grated turmeric)

½ tsp sea salt

½ tsp black peppercorns

1. In a medium saucepan, mix water (or broth), lemon slices, thyme, garlic, ginger, turmeric, salt, and peppercorns. Bring to a gentle simmer on medium-low heat.

2. Gently place the salmon fillets in a pan over low heat to poach. The liquid should be hot but not bubbling—like a spa treatment, not a boiling pot. Cover and allow to poach for 8-10 minutes, depending on thickness.

3. The salmon should be opaque and easily flaked with a fork. If necessary, poach for an additional minute or two.

4. Gently place the salmon on a plate. Drizzle with some extra virgin olive oil and a squeeze of fresh lemon. Garnish with additional herbs for a fresh finish.

Nom Nom your Way to not Feeling like Garbage | Irene Fields

Baked Cod with Mediterranean Flavors

Prep Time: 10 minutes

Cook Time: 15-18 minutes

Servings: 2 (1 fillet per person, about 6 oz each)

Pro Tip & Variation:

For extra flavor, add a splash of white wine before baking.

Want a spicy kick? Add red pepper flakes or smoked paprika.

For extra crunch, top with toasted pine nuts before serving.

Can't find cod? Try halibut, sea bass, or salmon instead.

2 wild-caught cod fillets (about 6 oz each)

1 cup cherry tomatoes, halved

¼ cup kalamata olives, sliced

1 tbsp extra virgin olive oil

2 garlic cloves, minced

½ tsp dried oregano

½ tsp ground turmeric

½ tsp sea salt

¼ tsp black pepper

1 tbsp capers

½ lemon, sliced into thin rounds

2 tbsp fresh parsley, chopped

1. Preheat your oven to 400°F (200°C). Lightly coat a baking dish with olive oil.

2. Layer the flavors. Place the cod fillets into the dish. Arrange the cherry tomatoes, olives, and capers around them. Drizzle everything with olive oil and season with garlic, oregano, turmeric, salt, and black pepper.

3. Place thin lemon slices over the cod. The acidity keeps the fish tender and complements the Mediterranean flavors.

4. Place the dish in the oven and bake for 15-18 minutes, or until the cod flakes easily with a fork.

5. Garnish with fresh parsley and serve immediately with quinoa, steamed greens, or a light arugula salad.

Nom Nom your Way to not Feeling like Garbage | **Irene Fields**

Grilled Mackerel with Ginger

Prep Time: 10 minutes

Cook Time: 8-10 minutes

Servings: 2 (1 fillet per person, about 6 oz each)

Pro Tips & Variations:

No grill? Use a hot cast-iron skillet or broil in the oven for a crispy finish.

Add more spice?

For extra crunch, add a pinch of red pepper flakes or drizzle with chili oil. Finish with toasted almonds or crushed peanuts.

No mackerel? Swap in sardines, trout, or salmon—just adjust the cooking time.

2 wild-caught mackerel fillets (about 6 oz each)

1 tbsp extra virgin olive oil

1-inch piece fresh ginger, grated

1 garlic clove, minced

½ tsp turmeric powder

1 tbsp low-sodium tamari (or coconut aminos for soy-free)

½ lime, juiced

¼ tsp black pepper

½ tsp sea salt

1 tsp honey

Garnish: chopped scallions, sesame seeds, or fresh cilantro

1. In a small mixing bowl, combine olive oil, grated ginger, garlic, turmeric, tamari, lime juice, black pepper, sea salt, and honey (if using).

2. Put the fillets in a shallow dish and pour the marinade over them. Allow them to sit for at least 10 minutes (or up to 30 minutes for a richer flavor).

3. Preheat the grill. Heat an outdoor grill or grill pan on medium-high heat. Lightly oil the grates to keep them from sticking.

4. Place the mackerel skin-side down and grill for 4-5 minutes per side, until crispy and flaky. Avoid flipping too frequently; just once is enough!

5. Transfer to a plate and garnish with chopped scallions, sesame seeds, or fresh cilantro for a fresh finish. Serve alongside steamed greens or a light cucumber salad.

Nom Nom your Way to not Feeling like Garbage | **Irene Fields**

Steamed Sea Bass with Asian Flavors

Prep Time: 10 minutes

Cook Time: 12-15 minutes

Servings: 2 (1 fillet per person, about 6 oz each)

Pro Tip & Variation:

No steamer? Use a large pan with a lid to elevate the fish with a small heatproof bowl inside.

For more umami, add fish sauce or toasted sesame seeds.

Additional crunch? Garnish with thinly sliced radishes or water chestnuts.

Other fish options include halibut, snapper, and trout.

2 wild-caught sea bass fillets (about 6 oz each)

1 tbsp fresh ginger, julienned

1 garlic clove, minced

2 tbsp low-sodium tamari (or coconut aminos for soy-free)

1 tbsp sesame oil (cold-pressed for the best flavor)

½ tsp turmeric powder

½ lime, juiced

2 tbsp scallions, thinly sliced

1 tbsp fresh cilantro, chopped

½ tsp red pepper flakes

¼ tsp sea salt

1. Prepare the steaming setup by filling a large pot or wok with about 2 inches of water and bringing it to a simmer. Put a steaming rack or heatproof plate inside.

2. Season the fish. Pat the sea bass fillets dry and place them on a heatproof plate that fits inside the steamer. Season with salt and turmeric powder, then top with ginger and garlic.

3. Steam the fish over medium heat for 12-15 minutes, or until tender and flaky with a fork.

4. To prepare the finishing sauce, combine tamari, sesame oil, lime juice, and red pepper flakes in a small bowl.

5. After cooking, carefully remove the fish from the steamer. Drizzle with sauce, then garnish with scallions and fresh cilantro. Serve immediately alongside steamed bok choy or cauliflower rice.

Nom Nom your Way to not Feeling like Garbage | **Irene Fields**

Grass-Fed Beef and Vegetable

Prep Time: 10 minutes

Cook Time: 10 minutes

Servings: 2 (About 2 cups per person)

Pro Tip & Variation:

For more umami, add fish sauce or miso paste.

For extra crunch, add shredded carrots or water chestnuts.

Choose a different protein? Try wild-caught shrimp or pasture-raised chicken instead of beef.

Serve in a bowl? Serve with quinoa or sautéed greens for added fiber.

Ingredients

- 8 oz grass-fed beef, thinly sliced (flank steak or sirloin works best)
- 1 tbsp extra virgin olive oil (or avocado oil)
- 1 garlic clove, minced
- 1-inch piece fresh ginger, grated
- ½ red bell pepper, thinly sliced
- ½ zucchini, cut into matchsticks
- ½ cup broccoli florets
- ½ cup snap peas
- 1 tbsp low-sodium tamari (or coconut aminos for soy-free)
- ½ tsp turmeric powder
- ¼ tsp black pepper
- ½ tsp red pepper flakes
- ½ lime, juiced
- 1 tbsp fresh cilantro, chopped
- Optional toppings: sesame seeds, crushed cashews, or hemp seeds

Instructions

1. In a bowl, combine the tamari, turmeric, black pepper, and lime juice. Toss in the beef slices and marinate while you prepare the vegetables (about 5-10 minute).

2. Heat 1 tbsp oil in a large skillet or wok on medium-high heat. Add the beef and sear for 2-3 minutes, or until browned. Remove from the pan and set aside.

3. Sauté aromatics in the same pan, adding more oil as needed. Mix in the garlic and ginger, stirring for 30 seconds until fragrant.

4. Cook the veggies, including bell pepper, zucchini, broccoli, and snap peas. Stir-fry for 3-4 minutes to keep them crisp-tender.

5. Return beef to the pan, add red pepper flakes, and toss for another minute to blend flavors.

6. Plate it and garnish with fresh cilantro, sesame seeds, or crushed cashews for extra crunch. Serve on its own or with cauliflower rice for a light and anti-inflammatory meal.

Stir-fry Slow-Cooked Beef and Sweet Potato Stew

Prep Time: 15 minutes

Cook Time: 4-6 hours (slow cooker) or 2 hours (stovetop)

Servings: 4 (About 1 ½ cups per person)

Pro Tip & Variation:

For a thicker stew, mash a few sweet potato chunks into the broth for a naturally creamy texture.

To add more greens, stir in kale or Swiss chard at the end. For a spicier kick, add cayenne or top with sliced chili peppers. Serve with cauliflower rice or quinoa for additional fiber.

For the Slow-Cooked Beef:

1 lb grass-fed beef chuck or stew meat, cut into chunks

1 tbsp extra virgin olive oil

2 cups bone broth (or low-sodium vegetable broth)

1 small onion, chopped

2 garlic cloves, minced

1-inch piece fresh ginger, grated

1 tsp turmeric powder

½ tsp black pepper

½ tsp cinnamon

½ tsp sea salt

½ lime, juiced

For the Stir-Fried Veggies & Sweet Potatoes:

1 medium sweet potato, peeled & cubed

½ red bell pepper, sliced

1 cup baby spinach

1 tbsp coconut oil or avocado oil

1 tsp coconut aminos or low-sodium tamari

½ tsp red pepper flakes

1 tbsp fresh cilantro, chopped

Slow Cooker Method (For Deep Flavor)

1. Sear the beef. Heat the olive oil in a skillet over medium-high heat. Sear the beef for 3-4 minutes, until browned on all sides.

2. Slow cook the magic. Place the beef in a slow cooker. Combine the broth, onion, garlic, ginger, turmeric, black pepper, cinnamon, salt, and lime juice. Stir well. Cover and cook until the beef is fork-tender, about 6 hours on low or 4 hours on high.

Stovetop Method (Faster and Just as Delicious)

1. Cook the beef in a heavy-bottomed pot with olive oil over medium-high heat.

Nom Nom your Way to not Feeling like Garbage | **Irene Fields**

2. Simmer it down. Combine the broth, onion, garlic, ginger, turmeric, cinnamon, black pepper, and salt. Bring to a boil, then lower heat to low, cover, and simmer for 1 ½ to 2 hours, until beef is tender.

Stir-fry vegetables and sweet potatoes.

1. Cook sweet potatoes. Heat the coconut oil in a large skillet over medium heat. Add sweet potatoes and sauté for 5-7 minutes, or until tender.

2. Include the bell pepper. Stir in the red bell pepper and cook for an additional 2 minutes, or until slightly softened.

3. Finish with spinach and seasonings. Combine baby spinach, coconut aminos, and red pepper flakes. Stir for 30 seconds, just until the spinach is wilted.

Bringing It All Together

1. If you prefer a shredded texture, use two forks to gently separate the beef.

2. Add the beef and its flavorful broth to the stir-fried vegetables and sweet potatoes. Stir thoroughly to coat everything in the rich sauce.

3. Top with fresh cilantro and serve warm

King Oyster Mushroom Scallops Tempeh Fish Fillets

Prep Time: 10 minutes

Cook Time: 10 minutes

Servings: 2 (About 6-8 "scallops" per person)

Pro Tip & Variation:

Looking for a seafood-like taste? Add a splash of seaweed broth or kelp powder.

For a buttery finish, use ghee instead of olive oil. Pair with roasted asparagus or miso-glazed bok choy..

4 king oyster mushrooms, stems only (cut into 1-inch thick rounds)

1 tbsp extra virgin olive oil (or avocado oil)

1 tbsp coconut aminos or low-sodium tamari

½ tsp turmeric powder

½ tsp smoked paprika (adds depth)

1 garlic clove, minced

½ lemon, juiced

¼ tsp black pepper

½ tsp sea salt

1 tbsp fresh parsley, chopped

1. In a small bowl, combine the coconut aminos, turmeric, smoked paprika, garlic, black pepper, salt, and lemon juice. Allow the mushroom rounds to marinate for at least 10 minutes (longer for deeper flavor).

2. To sear to perfection, heat olive oil in a pan over medium-high heat. Cook the mushroom "scallops" for 3-4 minutes per side, or until golden brown with a slight crust.

3. In the last minute of cooking, drizzle any remaining marinade over the mushrooms and allow to caramelize slightly.

4. Garnish with fresh parsley and serve alongside sautéed greens, quinoa, or a light citrus salad.

Nom Nom your Way to not Feeling like Garbage | **Irene Fields**

Tempeh "Fish" Fillets

Prep Time: 10 minutes

Cook Time: 12 minutes

Servings: 2 (1 fillet per person, about 4 oz each)

1 block organic tempeh (about 8 oz), cut into 2 thin fillets

1 tbsp extra virgin olive oil

1 tbsp coconut aminos (or low-sodium tamari)

½ tsp turmeric powder

½ tsp dulse flakes (or crumbled nori, for a mild seafood taste)

½ tsp smoked paprika

½ tsp garlic powder

½ tsp sea salt

¼ tsp black pepper

½ lemon, juiced

1 tbsp fresh dill or parsley, chopped

1. In a small mixing bowl, combine olive oil, grated ginger, garlic, turmeric, ta1. Steam the tempeh (optional but recommended).

To remove the bitterness, steam the tempeh in a small pot with 1 inch of water for 5 minutes before patting dry.

2. In a shallow dish, combine the olive oil, coconut aminos, turmeric, dulse flakes, smoked paprika, garlic powder, salt, black pepper, and lemon juice. Marinate the tempeh fillets for at least 10 minutes (or up to 30 minutes for a more intense flavor).

3. Preheat a pan over medium-high heat and lightly oil it. Cook the tempeh fillets for 5-6 minutes per side, or until crispy and golden.

4. To serve, garnish with fresh dill or parsley and a squeeze of lemon.mari, lime juice, black pepper, sea salt, and honey (if using).

2. Put the fillets in a shallow dish and pour the marinade over them. Allow them to sit for at least 10 minutes (or up to 30 minutes for a richer flavor).

3. Preheat the grill. Heat an outdoor grill or grill pan on medium-high heat. Lightly oil the grates to keep them from sticking.

Nom Nom your Way to not Feeling like Garbage | **Irene Fields**

4. Place the mackerel skin-side down and grill for 4-5 minutes per side, until crispy and flaky. Avoid flipping too frequently; just once is enough!

5. Transfer to a plate and garnish with chopped scallions, sesame seeds, or fresh cilantro for a fresh finish. Serve alongside steamed greens or a light cucumber salad.

Pro Tip & Variation:

For extra crispiness, coat with almond flour before pan-searing.

To enhance seafood flavor, add a splash of seaweed-infused broth to the marinade.

Pair it with roasted sweet potatoes or light fennel slaw.

Whole Grains and Pasta

Nom Nom your Way to not Feeling like Garbage | **Irene Fields**

Teff and vegetable pilaf

Prep Time: 10 minutes

Cook Time: 20 minutes

Servings: 2 (about 1 ½ cups per serving)

Pro Tip & Variation:

Increase the heartiness? Add cooked chickpeas or lentils.

For extra flavor, squeeze fresh lemon juice before serving.

Substitute bell peppers, mushrooms, or spinach.

Add smoked paprika or cayenne for extra flavor.

- ½ cup teff grain, rinsed
- 1 ¼ cups vegetable broth (or water)
- 1 tbsp extra virgin olive oil
- ½ small onion, finely chopped
- 1 garlic clove, minced
- ½ carrot, diced
- ½ zucchini, diced
- ½ tsp ground cumin
- ¼ tsp turmeric powder
- Pinch of black pepper
- ¼ tsp sea salt
- 2 tbsp chopped parsley
- 1 tbsp toasted pumpkin seeds

1. To sauté the aromatics, heat olive oil in a medium saucepan over medium heat. Add the onion and cook for 2 minutes, or until soft. Cook for an additional 2 minutes until the garlic, carrot, and zucchini are slightly tender.

2. To toast the teff, add the rinsed teff to the pan and stir for 30 seconds. This will enhance the nutty flavor.

3. Season with cumin, turmeric, black pepper, and salt. Stir to coat the grains and vegetables in the warm spices.

4. Add the broth, bring to a boil, and then reduce to a low heat. Cover and simmer for 15 minutes, or until the teff has absorbed the liquid.

5. Turn off the heat, cover for 5 minutes, and fluff with a fork. Stir in the chopped parsley and top with toasted pumpkin seeds for an extra anti-inflammatory crunch.

Nom Nom your Way to not Feeling like Garbage | Irene Fields

Red rice Mexican bowl

Prep Time: 10 minutes

Cook Time: 30 minutes

Servings: 2 (about 2 cups per serving)

For the Red Rice:

½ cup red rice, rinsed

1 cup vegetable broth (or water)

1 tbsp extra virgin olive oil

½ small onion, finely chopped

1 garlic clove, minced

½ tsp ground cumin

¼ tsp turmeric powder

½ cup fire-roasted diced tomatoes (canned or fresh)

Pinch of black pepper

¼ tsp sea salt

For the Bowl:

½ cup black beans, cooked

½ cup cherry tomatoes, halved

¼ avocado, sliced

2 tbsp chopped cilantro

1 tbsp toasted pumpkin seeds

1 tbsp fresh lime juice

1. Heat the olive oil in a medium saucepan over medium heat. Add the onion and sauté for 2 minutes, until soft.

2. Mix in the garlic, cumin, turmeric, black pepper, and salt. Cook for 30 seconds, until fragrant.

3. Add the rinsed red rice and stir to coat in the spices. Pour in the broth with the fire-roasted tomatoes.

4. Bring to a boil, then reduce the heat to low. Cover and simmer for 25-30 minutes, or until the rice is tender and the liquid has been absorbed.

Nom Nom your Way to not Feeling like Garbage | **Irene Fields**

Assemble the Bowl:

1. Fluff cooked red rice with a fork.

2. In a bowl, combine the red rice, black beans, cherry tomatoes, and avocado slices.

3. Add chopped cilantro and toasted pumpkin seeds. Drizzle with fresh lime juice.

Pro Tip & Variation:

Add more protein with grilled tempeh or fried egg.

For extra heat, add sliced jalapeños or hot sauce.

Swap the beans? Pinto or chickpeas are suitable.

Add crunch? Mix in shredded cabbage or radishes.

Amaranth porridge bowl

Prep Time: 5 minutes

Cook Time: 20 minutes

Servings: 1 (about 1 ½ cups per serving)

Pro Tip & Variation:

Want it thicker? Cook for a few minutes longer, or add another tablespoon of chia seeds.

Additional protein? Optional toppings include almond butter or plant-based protein powder. For added variety, try blueberries, hemp seeds, or cacao nibs.

Make it meal prep-friendly? Cook a large batch and refrigerate for up to four days.

¼ cup amaranth grains, rinsed

¾ cup unsweetened almond milk (or coconut milk)

½ cup water

½ tsp cinnamon

¼ tsp turmeric powder

Pinch of black pepper

½ tsp vanilla extract

1 tsp maple syrup (or raw honey)

Toppings:

¼ banana, sliced

1 tbsp crushed walnuts

1 tbsp chia seeds

1 tbsp unsweetened coconut flakes

1. In a small saucepan, heat the almond milk and water to a gentle boil. Mix in the rinsed amaranth, cinnamon, turmeric, and black pepper. Reduce the heat to low and simmer for 20 minutes, stirring occasionally, until thick and creamy.

2. Mix in the vanilla extract and maple syrup. Cook for an additional minute, then remove from heat.

3. To assemble the bowl, pour the porridge and top with sliced banana, walnuts, chia seeds, and coconut flakes.

Nom Nom your Way to not Feeling like Garbage | **Irene Fields**

Black rice Asian bowl

Prep Time: 10 minutes

Cook Time: 30 minutes

Servings: 2 (about 2 cups per serving)

Pro Tip & Variation:

Add more protein? Try grilled tofu, tempeh, or wild salmon.

For extra crunch, add roasted cashews or crushed nori.

For a spicy kick, drizzle with Sriracha or sprinkle with red pepper flakes.

For a warm dish, stir-fry the vegetables before adding to the bowl.

For the Black Rice:

½ cup black rice, rinsed

1 cup water or vegetable broth

½ tsp sea salt

For the Bowl:

½ cup edamame, cooked and shelled

½ cup red cabbage, thinly sliced

½ carrot, julienned or shredded

½ cucumber, sliced

1 tbsp toasted sesame seeds

2 tbsp chopped scallions

¼ avocado, sliced

For the Sesame-Ginger Dressing:

1 tbsp toasted sesame oil

1 tbsp tamari (or coconut aminos for soy-free)

1 tbsp rice vinegar

1 tsp fresh ginger, grated

1 tsp maple syrup (or raw honey)

½ tsp turmeric powder

½ tsp garlic, minced

1 tbsp water

1. Heat water (or broth) in a medium saucepan until it boils.

2. Combine the rinsed black rice and salt. Cover, reduce heat to low, and simmer for 25-30 minutes, until the liquid has been absorbed.

3. Fluff with a fork and allow to cool slightly.

To prepare the dressing, combine sesame oil, tamari, rice vinegar, ginger, maple syrup, turmeric, and garlic in a small bowl.

Assembling the Bowl:

1. Divide the cooked black rice between bowls.

2. Place the edamame, red cabbage, carrots, cucumber, and avocado on top.

3. Drizzle with the sesame ginger dressing.

Nom Nom your Way to not Feeling like Garbage | **Irene Fields**

4. Season with sesame seeds and scallions.

Wild Rice & Cranberry Pilaf

Prep Time: 10 minutes

Cook Time: 40 minutes

Servings: 2 (about 1 ½ cups per serving)

For the Wild Rice:

½ cup wild rice, rinsed

1 ½ cups vegetable broth (or water)

½ tsp sea salt

For the Pilaf:

1 tbsp extra virgin olive oil

½ small onion, finely chopped

1 celery stalk, diced

1 garlic clove, minced

½ tsp ground cinnamon

¼ tsp turmeric powder

¼ tsp black pepper

¼ cup dried cranberries (unsweetened, if possible)

¼ cup chopped walnuts (or pecans)

2 tbsp chopped parsley

1 tbsp fresh lemon juice

Cooking Wild Rice:

1. In a medium saucepan, heat the broth (or water) to a boil.

2. Add the rinsed wild rice and salt, then reduce the heat to low. Cover and cook for 35-40 minutes, until the rice is tender and the liquid has been absorbed.

3. Drain excess liquid as needed, then fluff with a fork.

Sauté Aromatics:

1. In a large pan, heat the olive oil over medium heat.

2. Add the onion and celery and cook for 3 minutes until soft.

3. Add garlic, cinnamon, turmeric, and black pepper, and cook for 30 seconds until fragrant.

Combine and Finish:

1. Toss the cooked wild rice in the pan to coat with the spices.

Nom Nom your Way to not Feeling like Garbage | **Irene Fields**

2. Mix in the cranberries, walnuts, parsley, and lemon juice.

3. Cook for another 2 minutes, stirring gently.

Pro Tip & Variation:

For a sweeter taste, add diced apple or pomegranate seeds.

To make it heartier, add cooked chickpeas or roasted sweet potatoes.

Want a nut-free option? Replace walnuts with pumpkin or sunflower seeds.

Looking for a flavor boost? A drizzle of balsamic glaze provides depth!

Spinach and chickpea curry with basmati rice

Prep Time: 10 minutes

Cook Time: 25 minutes

Servings: 2 (about 1 ½ cups curry + 1 cup rice per serving)

For the Curry:

1 tbsp extra virgin olive oil

½ small onion, finely chopped

1 garlic clove, minced

½ inch fresh ginger, grated

½ tsp cumin

½ tsp turmeric powder

½ tsp ground coriander

¼ tsp black pepper

½ cup diced tomatoes (fresh or canned)

½ cup coconut milk (full-fat for creaminess)

½ cup vegetable broth

1 cup cooked chickpeas (or ½ can, drained and rinsed)

2 cups fresh spinach, chopped

¼ tsp sea salt

½ tsp fresh lemon juice

For the Basmati Rice:

½ cup basmati rice, rinsed

1 cup water or vegetable broth

¼ tsp sea salt

Cook Basmati Rice:

1. In a small pot, heat the water (or broth) to a boil.

2. Stir in the rinsed rice and salt, then cover and reduce the heat to low.

3. Simmer for 12-15 minutes, then remove from the heat and cover for 5 minutes before fluffing with a fork.

Prepare the Curry:

1. Heat the olive oil in a medium-sized pan over medium heat. Add the onion and cook for 2 minutes until softened.

2. Mix in the garlic, ginger, cumin, turmeric, coriander, and black pepper. Cook for 30 seconds, until fragrant.

Nom Nom your Way to not Feeling like Garbage | **Irene Fields**

3. Add the diced tomatoes and cook for 3 minutes, stirring occasionally.

4. Add the coconut milk and vegetable broth, then stir in the chickpeas. Simmer for 10 minutes.

5. Add the chopped spinach and salt, and cook for another 2 minutes, until the spinach wilts.

6. Finish with a squeeze of lemon juice and remove from the heat.

Serve and enjoy:

Serve the curry with basmati rice and enjoy it warm!

Pro Tip & Variation:

Add extra protein with cubed tofu or tempeh.

For extra spice, add ¼ tsp cayenne or chili flakes.

For a creamier texture, blend half of the curry before serving.

To add more greens, replace spinach with kale or Swiss chard.

Spaghetti Squash Garlic Noodles

Prep Time: 10 minutes

Cook Time: 40 minutes (for roasting squash)

Servings: 2 (about 2 cups per serving)

For the Spaghetti Squash:

1 small spaghetti squash (about 2 lbs)

1 tbsp extra virgin olive oil

¼ tsp sea salt

¼ tsp black pepper

For the Garlic Sauce:

1 tbsp toasted sesame oil

2 garlic cloves, minced

1-inch fresh ginger, grated

2 tbsp tamari (or coconut aminos for soy-free)

1 tbsp rice vinegar

1 tsp maple syrup

½ tsp turmeric powder

½ tsp red pepper flakes

Toppings:

2 tbsp chopped cilantro

1 tbsp toasted sesame seeds

½ lime, cut into wedges

½ cup shredded carrots (for crunch)

½ cup sliced scallions

Roast the Spaghetti Squash

1. Preheat the oven to 400°F (200°C).

2. Cut the spaghetti squash in half lengthwise, then scoop out the seeds.

3. Drizzle with olive oil, season with salt and pepper, and place cut side down on a baking sheet.

4. Roast for 35-40 minutes, or until fork-tender. Allow to cool slightly before using a fork to scrape out the spaghetti-like strands.

Prepare the Garlic Sauce:

1. Heat the sesame oil in a pan over medium heat.

2. Sauté the garlic and ginger for 30 seconds, until fragrant.

Nom Nom your Way to not Feeling like Garbage | **Irene Fields**

3. Mix in the tamari, rice vinegar, maple syrup, turmeric, and red pepper flakes. Cook for one minute, then remove from heat.

Toss and Serve:

1. Add the spaghetti squash strands to the pan and toss to coat with the sauce.

2. Divide into bowls and garnish with shredded carrots, scallions, cilantro, and sesame seeds.

3. Serve with lime wedges and enjoy while warm!

Pro Tip & Variation:

Add more protein? Try edamame, grilled tofu, or shrimp.

For extra crunch, add roasted cashews or crushed peanuts.

To make a stir-fry, sauté the squash briefly before serving.

Add sautéed mushrooms or bok choy as an extra vegetable.

Farro Risotto With Butternut Squash and Kale

Prep Time: 10 minutes

Cook Time: 35 minutes

Servings: 2 (about 1 ½ cups per serving)

For the Butternut Squash:

1 cup butternut squash, diced

1 tbsp extra virgin olive oil

¼ tsp sea salt

¼ tsp black pepper

For the Farro Risotto:

½ cup farro, rinsed

1 tbsp extra virgin olive oil

½ small onion, finely chopped

1 garlic clove, minced

½ tsp turmeric powder

¼ tsp black pepper

2 cups vegetable broth, warmed

½ cup unsweetened almond milk (or oat milk for extra creaminess)

1 cup chopped kale, stems removed

1 tbsp nutritional yeast

½ tsp fresh thyme leaves

1 tbsp fresh lemon juice

Roast Butternut Squash:

1. Preheat the oven to 400°F (200°C).

2. Toss the diced butternut squash with olive oil, salt, and pepper.

3. Place on a baking sheet and roast for 20-25 minutes, flipping halfway through, until tender and caramelized.

Cook the Farro

1. Heat the olive oil in a large pan over medium heat.

2. Sauté the onion for 2 minutes, then add the garlic, turmeric, and black pepper. Cook for 30 seconds.

3. Stir in the farro, coating it with the aromatics.

Nom Nom your Way to not Feeling like Garbage | **Irene Fields**

4. Add ½ cup warm broth, stirring frequently until mostly absorbed. Repeat the process, adding broth ½ cup at a time until the farro is creamy and tender (approx. 25 minutes).

Add Finishing Touches:

1. Mix in the almond milk, chopped kale, roasted butternut squash, nutritional yeast, and thyme.

2. Cook for an additional 2-3 minutes, until the kale softens.

3. Remove from heat and add fresh lemon juice.

Pro Tip & Variation:

For extra creaminess, blend half the butternut squash before adding it.

Want more protein? Add toasted walnuts, hemp seeds, or chickpeas.

To make it richer, add a spoonful of tahini or cashew cream.

Different greens? Swap kale with spinach or Swiss chard.

Buckwheat noodle stir fry

Prep Time: 10 minutes

Cook Time: 15 minutes

Servings: 2 (about 2 cups per serving)

For the Stir-Fry:

4 oz buckwheat noodles (soba)

1 tbsp toasted sesame oil

½ small onion, thinly sliced

1 garlic clove, minced

1-inch fresh ginger, grated

½ cup broccoli florets

½ cup red bell pepper, julienned

½ cup carrot, shredded

½ cup snap peas, trimmed

½ cup shiitake mushrooms, sliced

1 cup baby spinach or bok choy, chopped

For the Sauce:

2 tbsp tamari (or coconut aminos for soy-free)

1 tbsp rice vinegar

1 tbsp maple syrup

½ tsp turmeric powder

¼ tsp black pepper

½ tsp red pepper flakes

1 tbsp water

Toppings:

1 tbsp sesame seeds

2 tbsp chopped scallions

½ lime, cut into wedges

1. Cook Buckwheat Noodles:

1. Bring a pot of water to a boil, then cook the noodles according to package directions (usually 4-5 minutes).

2. Drain and rinse with cold water to avoid sticking. Set aside.

Step 2: Stir-fry the vegetables.

1. Cook sesame oil in a large pan or wok over medium-high heat.

2. Combine the onion, garlic, and ginger. Sauté for 30 seconds, until fragrant.

3. Mix in the broccoli, bell pepper, carrots, snap peas, and mushrooms. Stir-fry for 3-4 minutes, until slightly tender but crisp.

Add Sauce and Noodles

Nom Nom your Way to not Feeling like Garbage | **Irene Fields**

1. In a small mixing bowl, combine tamari, rice vinegar, maple syrup, turmeric, black pepper, and red pepper flakes.

2. Place the cooked noodles and chopped spinach in the pan.

3. Pour in the sauce and toss everything together for 1-2 minutes, until thoroughly heated.

Serve and garnish:

1. Divide between bowls and garnish with sesame seeds and scallions.

2. Garnish with lime wedges and enjoy the warmth

Pro Tip & Variation:

Add more protein? Try tofu, tempeh, or edamame.

For extra crunch, add roasted cashews or slivered almonds.

For a heartier dish, add zucchini noodles or additional greens.

For a more umami flavor, add more mushrooms. Drizzle with some toasted sesame oil before serving.

Lentil and brown rice pilaf

Prep Time: 10 minutes

Cook Time: 35 minutes

Servings: 2 (about 1 ½ cups per serving)

½ cup brown rice, rinsed

½ cup green or brown lentils, rinsed

1 tbsp extra virgin olive oil

½ small onion, finely chopped

1 garlic clove, minced

½ tsp turmeric powder

¼ tsp ground cinnamon

¼ tsp black pepper

2 cups vegetable broth (or water)

½ tsp sea salt

¼ cup chopped fresh parsley

1 tbsp fresh lemon juice

¼ cup toasted almonds or walnuts

Sauté Aromatics:

1. Heat the olive oil in a medium pot over medium heat.

2. Add the onion and sauté for 2 minutes, until soft.

3. Mix in the garlic, turmeric, cinnamon, and black pepper. Cook for 30 seconds, until fragrant.

Cook the Pilaf

1. Add the rinsed brown rice and lentils to the pot and stir to coat with the spices.

2. Pour in the vegetable broth and bring to a boil.

3. Reduce the heat to low, cover, and cook for 30-35 minutes, or until the rice and lentils are tender and the liquid is absorbed.

Finish and serve:

1. Remove from heat and allow to sit for 5 minutes before fluffing with a fork.

2. Stir in the parsley and lemon juice.

Nom Nom your Way to not Feeling like Garbage | **Irene Fields**

3. Sprinkle it with toasted nuts for added crunch and nutrition.

Pro Tip & Variation:

Increase protein by adding cooked chickpeas or crumbled tempeh.

To make it heartier, add roasted sweet potatoes or sautéed mushrooms.

For a nut-free option, substitute pumpkin or sunflower seeds.

Want to add more flavor? Add a sprinkle of cumin or smoked paprika.

Soups and Stews

Nom Nom your Way to not Feeling like Garbage | **Irene Fields**

Warming Carrot & Tomato Soup

Prep Time: 10 minutes

Cook Time: 25 minutes

Servings: 2 (about 1 ½ cups per serving)

1 tbsp extra virgin olive oil

½ small onion, chopped

2 garlic cloves, minced

1-inch fresh ginger, grated

½ tsp turmeric powder

¼ tsp black pepper

½ tsp ground cumin

2 large carrots, peeled and chopped

1 cup diced tomatoes (fresh or canned)

2 cups vegetable broth

½ tsp sea salt

½ cup unsweetened coconut milk

1 tbsp fresh lemon juice

Toppings (Optional):

1 tbsp chopped fresh cilantro or parsley

1 tbsp toasted pumpkin seeds

A drizzle of extra virgin olive oil

Sauté the Aromatics:

1. Heat olive oil in a medium pot over medium heat.

2. Add onion, garlic, and ginger, sautéing for 2 minutes until fragrant.

3. Stir in turmeric, black pepper, and cumin, cooking for 30 seconds to toast the spices.

Simmer the Soup:

1. Add chopped carrots, diced tomatoes, vegetable broth, and salt.

2. Bring to a boil, then reduce heat and simmer for 15-20 minutes, until the carrots are soft.

Blend & Finish:

Nom Nom your Way to not Feeling like Garbage | **Irene Fields**

1. Use an immersion blender to purée the soup until smooth (or blend in batches in a blender).

2. Stir in coconut milk and lemon juice. Simmer for 2 more minutes, then remove from heat.

Serve & Garnish:

Ladle into bowls and top with fresh herbs, pumpkin seeds, or a drizzle of olive oil.

Pro Tips & Variations:

Want more protein? Stir in cooked lentils before blending.

Make it spicier? Add a pinch of cayenne or chili flakes.

More depth of flavor? Roast the carrots and tomatoes before adding them.

No coconut milk? Use almond milk or cashew cream for creaminess.

Turnip and Fennel Soup

Prep Time: 10 minutes

Cook Time: 25 minutes

Servings: 2 (about 1 ½ cups per serving)

1 tbsp extra virgin olive oil

½ small onion, chopped

1 garlic clove, minced

½ fennel bulb, sliced (save some fronds for garnish!)

2 medium turnips, peeled and chopped

½ tsp turmeric powder

¼ tsp black pepper

¼ tsp ground cumin (adds warmth)

2 cups vegetable broth

½ cup unsweetened almond milk (or coconut milk for extra creaminess)

½ tsp sea salt

1 tbsp fresh lemon juice

Toppings (Optional):

Fennel fronds, chopped

Toasted pumpkin seeds or walnuts

A drizzle of extra virgin olive oil

Sauté the Aromatics:

1. Heat olive oil in a medium pot over medium heat.

2. Add onion and garlic, sautéing for 2 minutes until fragrant.

3. Stir in fennel, turnips, turmeric, black pepper, and cumin. Cook for 3 minutes to soften.

Simmer the Soup:

1. Pour in vegetable broth and bring to a boil.

2. Reduce heat and simmer for 15-20 minutes, until turnips are tender.

Blend & Finish:

1. Use an immersion blender to purée the soup until smooth (or blend in batches).

2. Stir in almond milk and lemon juice. Simmer for 2 more minutes, then remove from heat.

Nom Nom your Way to not Feeling like Garbage | **Irene Fields**

Serve & Garnish:

Ladle into bowls, top with fennel fronds, toasted seeds, and a drizzle of olive oil.

Pro Tips & Variations:

Want more protein? Stir in cooked white beans before blending.

Make it heartier? Add a diced potato for extra creaminess.

More depth of flavor? Roast the turnips and fennel before adding.

No almond milk? Use oat milk or cashew cream.

Nom Nom your Way to not Feeling like Garbage | **Irene Fields**

Moroccan-Spiced Squash Soup

Prep Time: 10 minutes

Cook Time: 30 minutes

Servings: 2 (about 1 ½ cups per serving))

- 1 tbsp extra virgin olive oil
- ½ small onion, chopped
- 2 garlic cloves, minced
- 1-inch fresh ginger, grated
- ½ tsp ground cumin
- ½ tsp ground coriander
- ½ tsp turmeric powder
- ¼ tsp cinnamon (adds warmth)
- ¼ tsp black pepper
- 2 cups butternut squash, peeled & cubed
- 2 cups vegetable broth
- ½ cup unsweetened coconut milk
- ½ tsp sea salt
- 1 tbsp fresh lemon juice

Toppings (Optional):

- Chopped fresh cilantro or parsley
- Toasted pumpkin seeds
- A drizzle of extra virgin olive oil

Sauté the Aromatics:

1. Heat olive oil in a medium pot over medium heat.

2. Add onion and sauté for 2 minutes until soft.

3. Stir in garlic, ginger, cumin, coriander, turmeric, cinnamon, and black pepper. Cook for 30 seconds until fragrant.

Simmer the Soup:

1. Add butternut squash and vegetable broth. Bring to a boil.

2. Reduce heat and let simmer for 20-25 minutes, until squash is tender.

Blend & Finish:

1. Use an immersion blender to purée the soup until smooth (or blend in batches).

Nom Nom your Way to not Feeling like Garbage | **Irene Fields**

2. Stir in coconut milk and lemon juice. Simmer for 2 more minutes, then remove from heat.

Serve & Garnish:

Ladle into bowls and top with fresh cilantro, toasted pumpkin seeds, or a drizzle of olive oil.

Pro Tips & Variations:

Want extra protein? Stir in cooked chickpeas before blending.

Make it heartier? Add a diced carrot or sweet potato.

More spice? Add a pinch of cayenne or smoked paprika.

No coconut milk? Use almond milk or cashew cream for creaminess.

Butternut Squash Thai Curry

Prep Time: 10 minutes

Cook Time: 30 minutes

Servings: 2 (about 1 ½ cups per serving)

1 tbsp coconut oil

½ small onion, chopped

2 garlic cloves, minced

1-inch fresh ginger, grated

1 tbsp Thai red curry paste

½ tsp turmeric powder

¼ tsp black pepper

2 cups butternut squash, peeled & cubed

1 cup red bell pepper, sliced

1 ½ cups vegetable broth

1 cup unsweetened coconut milk

½ cup chickpeas

1 tbsp fresh lime juice

½ tsp sea salt

1 tbsp coconut aminos (or tamari)

Toppings (Optional):

Fresh cilantro or Thai basil

Toasted cashews or peanuts

Sliced red chili (for extra heat)

Sauté the Aromatics:

1. Heat coconut oil in a large pan over medium heat.

2. Add onion and sauté for 2 minutes until soft.

3. Stir in garlic, ginger, red curry paste, turmeric, and black pepper. Cook for 30 seconds until fragrant.   Cook the Curry:

1. Add butternut squash, bell pepper, and vegetable broth.

2. Bring to a boil, then reduce heat and let simmer for 15 minutes, until squash is fork-tender.

Add the Coconut Milk & Chickpeas:

1. Stir in coconut milk, chickpeas, lime juice, salt, and coconut aminos.

Nom Nom your Way to not Feeling like Garbage | Irene Fields

2. Simmer for another 5 minutes until flavors meld.

Serve & Garnish:

Ladle into bowls and top with fresh herbs, toasted nuts, and sliced chili. Serve with jasmine rice or cauliflower rice.

Pro Tips & Variations:

Want more protein? Add tofu or tempeh.

Make it heartier? Stir in spinach or kale at the end.

More heat? Add extra Thai red curry paste or chili flakes.

No coconut milk? Use cashew cream or almond milk for a lighter version.

Spiced Pumpkin & Split Pea Soup

Prep Time: 10 minutes

Cook Time: 40 minutes

Servings: 2 (about 1 ½ cups per serving)

1 tbsp extra virgin olive oil

½ small onion, chopped

2 garlic cloves, minced

1 inch fresh ginger, grated

½ cup yellow or green split peas, rinsed

1 cup pumpkin purée (canned or fresh roasted)

½ tsp turmeric powder

¼ tsp black pepper

½ tsp ground cumin

¼ tsp ground cinnamon (adds warmth)

½ tsp sea salt

2 ½ cups vegetable broth

½ cup unsweetened coconut milk

1 tbsp fresh lemon juice

Toppings (Optional):

Fresh cilantro or parsley

Toasted pumpkin seeds

A drizzle of extra virgin olive oil

Sauté the Aromatics:

1. Heat olive oil in a medium pot over medium heat.

2. Add onion and sauté for 2 minutes until soft.

3. Stir in garlic, ginger, turmeric, cumin, cinnamon, and black pepper. Cook for 30 seconds until fragrant.

Cook the Soup:

1. Add rinse split peas and vegetable broth. Bring to a boil.

2. Reduce heat and let simmer for 30 minutes, until split peas are soft.

3. Stir in pumpkin purée, salt, and coconut milk. Simmer for 5 more minutes.

Blend & Finish:

1. Use an immersion blender to purée the soup until smooth (or blend in batches).

2. Stir in fresh lemon juice and adjust seasoning if needed.

Serve & Garnish:

Ladle into bowls and top with fresh herbs, pumpkin seeds, or a drizzle of olive oil. Enjoy the warmth!

Pro Tips & Variations:**

Want extra protein? Add cooked lentils or quinoa.

Make it heartier? Stir in chopped kale or spinach at the end.

More spice? Add a pinch of cayenne or smoked paprika.

No coconut milk? Use almond milk or cashew cream for creaminess.

Mexican-Style Pinto Bean Soup

Prep Time: 10 minutes

Cook Time: 30 minutes

Servings: 2 (about 1 ½ cups per serving)

1 tbsp extra virgin olive oil

½ small onion, chopped

2 garlic cloves, minced

1 small carrot, diced

½ small bell pepper, diced

½ tsp ground cumin

½ tsp turmeric powder

½ tsp smoked paprika

¼ tsp black pepper

¼ tsp ground oregano

1 cup cooked pinto beans (or ½ can, drained and rinsed)

2 cups vegetable broth

½ cup diced tomatoes (fresh or canned)

½ tsp sea salt

½ tsp lime juice (freshly squeezed)

Toppings (Optional):

Fresh cilantro

Sliced avocado

Toasted pumpkin seeds

A drizzle of extra virgin olive oil

Sauté the Aromatics:

1. Heat olive oil in a medium pot over medium heat.

2. Add onion, garlic, carrot, and bell pepper. Sauté for 3 minutes until softened.

3. Stir in cumin, turmeric, smoked paprika, black pepper, and oregano. Cook for 30 seconds until fragrant.

Simmer the Soup:

1. Add pinto beans, vegetable broth, diced tomatoes, and salt. Bring to a boil.

2. Reduce heat and let simmer for 20-25 minutes, allowing flavors to meld.

Blend & Finish:

1. Mash some of the beans with the back of a spoon for a thicker texture (or blend a small portion for a creamier consistency).

2. Stir in fresh lime juice.

Serve & Garnish:

Ladle into bowls and top with fresh cilantro, sliced avocado, or pumpkin seeds. Enjoy warm with tortillas or brown rice

Pro Tips & Variations:

Want extra protein? Add quinoa or cooked lentils.

Make it heartier? Stir in chopped kale or spinach at the end.

More spice? Add a pinch of chili flakes or a chopped jalapeño.

No pinto beans? Use black beans or red kidney beans.

Mung Bean & Green Vegetable Soup

Prep Time: 10 minutes

Cook Time: 30 minutes

Servings: 2 (about 1 ½ cups per serving)

- 1 tbsp extra virgin olive oil
- ½ small onion, chopped
- 2 garlic cloves, minced
- 1-inch fresh ginger, grated
- ½ tsp turmeric powder
- ½ tsp ground cumin
- ¼ tsp black pepper
- ¼ tsp ground coriander
- ½ cup dried mung beans, rinsed and soaked for 2 hours (or overnight)
- 3 cups vegetable broth
- ½ zucchini, diced
- 1 cup chopped spinach (or kale)
- ½ tsp sea salt
- ½ tsp fresh lemon juice

Toppings (Optional):

- Fresh cilantro or parsley
- Toasted pumpkin seeds or sesame seeds
- A drizzle of extra virgin olive oil

Sauté the Aromatics:

1. Heat olive oil in a medium pot over medium heat.

2. Add onion, garlic, and ginger, sautéing for 2 minutes until fragrant.

3. Stir in turmeric, cumin, black pepper, and coriander. Cook for 30 seconds to toast the spices.

Cook the Mung Beans:

1. Add mung beans and vegetable broth. Bring to a boil.

2. Reduce heat and let simmer for 20 minutes, until the beans are soft.

Add the Vegetables:

1. Stir in zucchini, spinach, and salt. Simmer for 5 more minutes, until tender.

Nom Nom your Way to not Feeling like Garbage | **Irene Fields**

Blend & Finish (Optional):

1. For a creamy texture, blend half the soup with an immersion blender.

2. Stir in fresh lemon juice.

Serve & Garnish:

Ladle into bowls and top with fresh herbs, seeds, or a drizzle of olive oil.

Pro Tips & Variations:

Want extra protein? Add cooked quinoa or lentils.

Make it heartier? Stir in coconut milk for extra creaminess.

More spice? Add a pinch of chili flakes or a chopped green chili.

No mung beans? Use lentils or split peas.

Chickpea Sweet Potato Stew

Prep Time: 10 minutes

Cook Time: 30 minutes

Servings: 2 (about 1 ½ cups per serving)

- 1 tbsp extra virgin olive oil
- ½ small onion, chopped
- 2 garlic cloves, minced
- 1-inch fresh ginger, grated
- ½ tsp ground cumin
- ½ tsp turmeric powder
- ½ tsp smoked paprika
- ¼ tsp black pepper
- ¼ tsp cinnamon (adds depth)
- 1 small sweet potato, peeled and cubed (about 1 cup)
- 1 cup cooked chickpeas (or ½ can, drained and rinsed)
- 1 ½ cups vegetable broth
- ½ cup diced tomatoes (fresh or canned)
- ½ tsp sea salt
- ½ cup unsweetened coconut milk
- 1 tbsp fresh lemon juice

Toppings (Optional):

- Fresh cilantro or parsley
- Toasted pumpkin seeds or chopped almonds
- A drizzle of extra virgin olive oil

Sauté the Aromatics:

1. Heat olive oil in a medium pot over medium heat.

2. Add onion, garlic, and ginger. Sauté for 2 minutes until fragrant.

3. Stir in cumin, turmeric, smoked paprika, black pepper, and cinnamon. Cook for 30 seconds to release the spices' flavors.

Simmer the Stew:

1. Add sweet potatoes, chickpeas, vegetable broth, diced tomatoes, and salt. Stir well.

2. Bring to a boil, then reduce heat and simmer for 20-25 minutes, until sweet potatoes are soft.

Nom Nom your Way to not Feeling like Garbage | **Irene Fields**

Add Coconut Milk & Finish:

1. Stir in coconut milk and let simmer for 5 more minutes.

2. Remove from heat and stir in fresh lemon juice.

Serve & Garnish:

Ladle into bowls and top with fresh herbs, toasted seeds, or a drizzle of olive oil. Serve with warm whole-grain bread or brown rice.

Pro Tips & Variations:

Want extra protein? Add cooked quinoa or lentils.

Make it heartier? Stir in chopped kale or spinach at the end.

More spice? Add a pinch of chili flakes or a diced green chili.

No coconut milk? Use almond milk or cashew cream for a lighter version.

CHAPTER 9

Cortisol Detox

Alright, let's dissect this since knowing how cortisol works is like opening the stress response's hidden handbook. And trust me, it's much simpler to accept yourself and start making positive changes once you know what's happening behind the scenes.

Although cortisol is frequently referred to as the "stress hormone," this term does not adequately capture its actual meaning. It functions more like your body's natural energy regulator and alarm system, produced by your adrenal glands, which are tiny but mighty organs situated above your kidneys. Your body releases cortisol to help you cope with danger, whether it's a genuine threat or a passive-aggressive email from your boss.

In moderation, cortisol can be helpful. It balances blood pressure, lowers inflammation, controls your metabolism, and even your sleep-wake cycle. It increases your vitality, sharpens your focus, and primes your body for combat or escape. Very helpful if you're, say, trying to avoid a bear. Not very useful if you're just fuming and stuck in traffic.

The Impact of Stress on Hormones and Metabolism

The catch is this: Life-threatening events and routine stressors like deadlines, childcare chaos, or scrolling through bad news on your phone are indistinguishable to your body. Therefore, when you're under a lot of stress, your cortisol levels stay high, which is when things start to go wrong.

Your entire hormone system is upset when your cortisol levels are consistently elevated. Blood sugar spikes and crashes as a result of its interference with insulin (hello, cravings). It disrupts your cycle, interferes with progesterone and estrogen, and aggravates perimenopausal symptoms and PMS. Additionally, it instructs your body to store fat as a survival strategy, especially around your stomach.

There is also a negative impact on metabolism. Your body stays in "store mode," assuming famine or calamity is on the horizon, rather than burning fat for energy. Even if everything is "right," you might still feel more hungry, gain weight more quickly, and struggle to gain muscle mass.
Healthy and unhealthy cortisol levels.

So, what does cortisol balance look like? Your cortisol levels should ideally follow a natural cycle, peaking in the morning to help you wake up, progressively dropping throughout the day, and through out at night to enable restful sleep.

Nom Nom your Way to not Feeling like Garbage | Irene Fields

However, this rhythm is upset when stress is constant. You might feel wired but exhausted, anxious, easily agitated, have trouble falling asleep, and have stubborn belly fat if you have too much cortisol.

Constant fatigue, trouble getting out of bed, dependence on caffeine for energy, and emotional numbness are symptoms of low cortisol levels.

What's the good news? With the correct lifestyle adjustments, stress-reduction strategies, and lots of self-compassion, cortisol levels can be balanced. Learning to manage your cortisol levels is a big step toward feeling calm, energized, and genuinely well. You don't have to live in constant stress.

High Cortisol Symptoms (And How to Identify Them Early)

Have you ever experienced fatigue, mental haze, and inexplicable sugar cravings that make you feel like you're dragging through life? Instead of "normal" stress or burnout, it's possible that your cortisol is taking over. Additionally, you can start to turn things around sooner if you notice the warning signs.

Let's dissect it.

- ✓ Persistent weariness and problems. Dozing off
- ✓ Feeling exhausted all the time, even when you think you're getting enough sleep, is one of the most subtle indicators of high cortisol. In order to wake you up, cortisol usually peaks in the morning and then progressively decreases throughout the day. However, this rhythm is upset when cortisol levels stay high, leaving you wired at night and groggy in the morning.
- ✓ You might be unable to unwind and lie in bed for hours.
- ✓ Throughout the night, get up multiple times.
- ✓ No matter how much you sleep, you will still feel unrefreshed.

This cycle is cruel: Cortisol is raised by poor sleep, and sleep is disturbed by high cortisol. Don't worry, though; later in the book, we'll go over how to reset your rhythm.

Weight gain, especially around the abdomen, and sugar cravings

Your body might require a cortisol reset if you have a persistent craving for salty or sweet snacks. Blood sugar imbalances brought on by high cortisol levels make you crave rapid energy boosts. Additionally, as part of your body's long-standing survival mechanism, cortisol encourages the storage of fat, especially around the midsection.

The issue is not one of self-control or "eating better." Your biology is trying to keep you alive in response to ongoing stress. What's the good news? You may experience an improvement in your cravings and stubborn weight once you begin reducing your cortisol levels.

Brain fog, agitation, and anxiety

Have you ever had the feeling that your brain was unable to keep up with your emotions, or that they were riding a rollercoaster? Your mood and cognitive abilities may be unexpectedly impacted by high cortisol levels.

Keep an eye out for these indicators:
- ✓ Raced thoughts or ongoing anxiety
- ✓ Yelling at family members over trivial matters.
- ✓ Difficulty focusing or recalling specifics.

Neurotransmitters that control mood and focus, like dopamine and serotonin, interact with cortisol. Therefore, you might feel frazzled and mentally hazy when your cortisol levels are off.
Low libido, irregular periods, and hormonal imbalances.

Your entire hormonal system may be disrupted by elevated cortisol levels, which have an impact beyond your stress response. Your body puts survival ahead of reproductive health when it is in a persistent fight-or-flight state.

This may show up as:
- ✓ Period irregularities or absences
- ✓ Enhanced symptoms of perimenopause or PMS

Vaginal dryness or low sexual drive

Although it's annoying, you can move from self-blame to self-care by understanding that this is how your body handles stress. What's the best part? Your hormones can often return to balance on their own when cortisol levels are balanced.

The Hidden Stressors

An impending deadline or a busy morning with the kids are two examples of situations where stress is evident. It can occasionally infiltrate through routines and habits that we are unaware of. Let's examine a few of the obscure cortisol triggers that might be throwing off your equilibrium.

How to Wean Off of Sugar, Caffeine, and Alcohol

Everyone has vices, don't we? Coffee to start the day, a sweet treat to increase energy, and a glass of wine to relax. These small pleasures, however, have the potential to quickly raise and lower your cortisol levels.

Although alcohol may seem to be calming, it actually increases cortisol levels and interferes with sleep, which makes you feel more exhausted and stressed the following day.

- ✓ Caffeine: Excessive cortisol production from your favorite coffee is okay in moderation, but chronic over-caffeination keeps your body alert all the time.

- ✓ Sugar: Each drop in blood sugar causes an increase in cortisol to raise your levels again, and those brief spikes in energy are followed by a crash.

Going cold turkey (unless you want to) is not the aim. It all comes down to making small adjustments and practicing mindful moderation: cutting back on caffeine, switching to whole-food sugar substitutes, and finding new ways to relax without drinking.

Negative news exposure, social media, and doom scrolling

Have you ever caught yourself in an Instagram comparison trap or felt your chest tighten while reading through unfavorable news? Even if you're just sitting on the couch, your stress response is already in motion.

- ✓ Constant news cycles and social media can: Flood your brain with negativity that raises cortisol levels makes you feel overstimulated and "on" all the time.
- ✓ Emotional stress from feelings of inadequacy raises cortisol levels.

This is where setting limits changes everything. Establish "no-phone" hours, try social media detoxes, and curate your feeds to feature upbeat, uplifting content.

Stress from money and the need to "do it all"

Your reserves can be subtly depleted by financial concerns and social expectations. Your cortisol levels may remain high due to the ongoing pressure to be a responsible parent, a powerhouse at work, and to keep everything running smoothly.

- ✓ Financial anxiety: Your fight-or-flight reaction may be triggered by worries about bills, debt, or the future.
- ✓ Overcommitment and Perfectionism: Your nervous system is always on high alert when you feel the need to succeed in every area of your life.

To deal with this, one must develop self-compassion, learn to set boundaries, and take proactive, small steps to reduce emotional and financial strains without being burdened by irrational expectations.

Absence of connection and physical touch

Although meaningful touch and presence can be scarce in today's fast-paced, screen-heavy world, human connection is a natural cortisol regulator.

Hugs and handshakes are examples of physical affection that lowers cortisol and raises oxytocin, the "love hormone". However, a lot of women go for extended periods of time without being cared for, particularly if they are unmarried, live alone, or are always "on" for other people without getting care for themselves.

Easy methods to bring this back into your life:

- ✓ There is science behind this, so give your loved ones a hug for at least 20 seconds!
- ✓ Hug your pets or get a soothing massage.
- ✓ Make in-person time with friends a priority, even for brief, informal get-togethers.

Not all connections need to come from other people; you can relax your nervous system by massaging yourself, doing light stretches, or putting your hand on your heart when you're feeling stressed.

Resetting Your Nervous System and Entering Parasympathetic Mode

Teaching your body to shift out of fight-or-flight mode is another aspect of cortisol balance, in addition to stress management. Chronic stress can be countered by learning to consciously activate your parasympathetic nervous system, also referred to as your "rest and digest" mode.

Let's examine the methods that help your body enter this healing state gradually.

When you're totally absorbed in something you love, like journaling, painting, dancing, or gardening, you're said to be in a "flow state." Your body naturally relaxes, your mind becomes calm, and your cortisol levels decrease when you're in flow.

To determine your flow:
- ✓ Embrace your curiosity. What kinds of things thrill you or bring back your childhood?
- ✓ Remove the pressure: Flow is about being present, not about being productive.
- ✓ Create a play area: Your nervous system can be reset by just doing something for fun for even twenty minutes.
- ✓ Your brain takes a little vacation when your nervous system is happy, creative, and focused.

A quick and easy technique to instantly calm your system is 4-7-8 breathing.

Your breathing becomes shallow when your stress response is triggered. How can you give your body a safety signal the quickest? Breathe deliberately and slowly.

The 4-7-8 breath changes everything:
- ✓ Take a four-second breath.
- ✓ Hold for seven seconds.
- ✓ Take an eight-second breath out.
- ✓ To lower your heart rate, relax your muscles, and clear your head, repeat this four times. Resetting your stress response is similar to doing that.

The Wim Hof Method: Developing Resilience through Breathwork and Cold Therapy
Although it may seem drastic, exposure to cold is a useful technique for conditioning your nervous system to cope with stress. Your body gains resilience and learns to control cortisol when you purposefully expose yourself to cold (for instance, by taking an ice bath or a cold shower).

Try it out:
- ✓ Start small: Use cold water for 30 seconds to end your shower.
- ✓ Combine with breathwork. You can stay composed in the cold by breathing deeply and deliberately.
- ✓ Honor the Afterglow: Your body is flooded with endorphins and relaxation after being exposed to cold.

This exercise can help you become more resilient to stress over time, which will speed up your body's recovery from cortisol surges.

Sauna, Cold Showers, and Physical Stress Reduction
Not only are heat and cold treatments fashionable, but they also aid in your body's stress adaptation. Saunas release endorphins, promote relaxation, and enhance circulation. A hormetic stress response is triggered by cold showers and ice baths, teaching your body how to bounce back from discomfort. You can try contrast therapy, which alternates between heat and cold, if you have access to a sauna.

Reduced cortisol levels at baseline
Boost your energy and mood.
Boost your recuperation and sleep.
Your nervous system can receive a signal of safety from even basic at-home activities, like taking an Epsom salt bath or getting some fresh air.

Your body learns that it's acceptable to relax each time you intentionally engage your parasympathetic nervous system. These techniques are long-term strategies for reducing cortisol, enhancing resilience, and fostering inner peace rather than just short-term stress relief.

CHAPTER 10

The Food Elimination Plan for Anti-Inflammation

If you've ever experienced joint pain, fatigue, bloating, or brain fog, you may have chronic inflammation, and the food you eat could be exacerbating the problem. When I first started my anti-inflammatory journey, I had no idea how much certain foods were causing my symptoms. I was eating foods I thought were healthy, but they were actually causing inflammation in my body.

This is where the Food Elimination Plan comes in. It isn't about deprivation; it's about discovery. By temporarily eliminating common inflammatory foods, you can determine what is truly affecting your body and create a diet that makes you feel your best.

Let's look at the science behind it, which foods to eliminate, and how to reintroduce foods without causing inflammation.

Why Eliminate Specific Foods?

IF your body's natural defense mechanism, designed to fight infections and heal injuries. However, when inflammation becomes chronic, it turns against you and causes conditions such as:
- ✓ Autoimmune diseases: rheumatoid arthritis, lupus, Hashimoto's.
- ✓ Digestive Issues (IBS, Crohn's, Bloating)
- ✓ Skin conditions: eczema, psoriasis, acne
- ✓ Metabolic disorders include obesity, diabetes, and heart disease
- ✓ Mood swings, brain fog, fatigue

Certain foods are triggers, causing your immune system to overreact, resulting in leaky gut, insulin resistance, and oxidative stress. An elimination plan aims to identify your specific triggers and replace them with nourishing, healing foods.

Step 1: Foods To Eliminate (The Usual Suspects)

For 3 to 6 weeks, you should avoid all potential inflammatory foods. These are the largest culprits.

1. Processed and Refined Foods: These foods contain preservatives, additives, and unhealthy fats that cause inflammation.
   * Avoid consuming fast food, packaged snacks, chips, and processed meats. Artificial sweeteners, food dyes, and MSG

- 2. Sugar and Refined Carbs: Excess sugar spikes insulin levels, causing chronic inflammation and increasing the risk of diabetes
- Soda, fruit juices, candy, and pastries
- White bread, pasta, and white rice.

3. Industrial Seed Oil: vegetable, soybean, and canola oil contain high levels of omega-6 fatty acids, which promote inflammation.
- Vegetable, soybean, and corn oils
- Margarine and shortening

4. Dairy: Some individuals may experience digestive distress and inflammation due to lactose and casein sensitivities.
- Milk, cheese, butter, yogurt (alternatives include coconut yogurt).

5) Gluten and Grains: Even if you are not gluten-intolerant, gluten can increase gut permeability (leaky gut), which causes inflammation.
- Avoid wheat, barley, rye, and oats unless certified gluten-free. Pasta, bread, and crackers

6. Legumes and Nightshades (For Some People): Some people, especially those with autoimmune issues, may experience worsening inflammation due to the presence of lectins and saponins.
- Soy, peanuts, lentils, and beans. Tomatoes, potatoes, peppers and eggplant

7. Alcohol: Alcohol disrupts gut bacteria, causes liver stress, and promotes systemic inflammation.
- Beer, wine, and liquor.

Excess caffeine can increase cortisol levels, causing chronic stress and inflammation.
- Coffee, energy drinks, and caffeine-rich teas

Step 2: What to Eat Instead (Healing Foods)

While eliminating inflammatory foods, concentrate on nourishing, anti-inflammatory alternatives.

1. Healthful Fats (Omega-3s and monounsaturated fats).
✓ Avocados, olive oil and coconut oil.
✓ Wild-caught salmon, sardines, and mackerel.
✓ Nuts and seeds: walnuts, flaxseeds, and chia seeds.

2. Anti-inflammatory proteins
✓ Organic poultry and pasture-raised meats
✓ Wild-caught fish high in omega-3s
✓ Bone broth for gut health

Nom Nom your Way to not Feeling like Garbage | **Irene Fields**

3. Foods That Heal the Gut
✓ Consume fermented foods (sauerkraut, kimchi, kefir, coconut yogurt) and probiotic-rich foods (miso, kombucha).
✓ Collagen and gelatin help repair leaky gut.

4. Low Glycemic Fruits and Vegetables
✓ Leafy greens (kale, spinach, Swiss chard)
✓ Cruciferous vegetables (broccoli, Brussels sprouts, cauliflower).
✓ Berries, citrus, and apples

5. Herbs and Spices (Nature's Medicine)
✓ Turmeric, ginger, cinnamon, garlic, and oregano

Step 3: Reintroducing Foods (Testing for Triggers)

After 3 to 6 weeks, gradually reintroduce eliminated foods one at a time to determine which ones your body can tolerate.

How to Reintroduce Foods
✓ Start with one food at a time, for example, dairy.
✓ Eat for 2-3 days, then stop. Track symptoms for up to a week.
✓ Look for signs of inflammation:
- Digestive problems (bloating, gas, cramps).
- Possible side effects include skin reactions (rashes, acne, eczema), fatigue, joint pain, and headaches.
✓ If symptoms occur, eliminate the food again. If no reaction occurs, it is probably safe to take in moderation.

Step 4: Long-Term Anti-inflammatory Eating

After determining your trigger foods, you can create a long-term anti-inflammatory lifestyle by:

- Prioritize whole, nutrient-dense foods.
- Balance healthy fats (omega-3s) with minimal omega-6s.
- Reduce sugar and processed foods.
- Eat gut-friendly foods.
- Manage stress, improve sleep, and stay active.

The goal is not perfection; it is listening to your body and developing a diet that allows you to thrive.

My Experience with Food Elimination
Nom Nom your Way to not Feeling like Garbage | **Irene Fields**

When I first tried this method, I was skeptical. After just a few weeks, I noticed:
- ✓ Less bloating and stomach discomfort
- ✓ More energy and fewer afternoon crashes
- ✓ Clearer skin and fewer headaches
- ✓ No more morning joint pain

I realized that my body felt best without dairy and gluten, but I could tolerate small amounts of legumes without difficulty. Now, my diet is tailored to what works for me, which is the beauty of this approach: it is completely personalized to you.

If you're tired of feeling sluggish, inflamed, and out of sync with your body, this plan could be the solution. It's not just about eliminating foods; it's also about understanding your body's specific needs and learning to eat in a way that supports healing and long-term vitality.

4 WEEKS MEAL PLAN

Week 1

Monday

Breakfast: Spinach & Egg Scramble (p.27)
Lunch: Kale and Quinoa Salad (p.44)
Dinner: Poached Salmon with Herbs (p.69)
Snack: Chia Pudding with Flax, Hemp & Goji Berries (p.42)

Tuesday

Breakfast: Avocado & Kale Omelet (p.28)
Lunch: Arugula and Beet Salad (p.46)
Dinner: Grilled Mackerel with Ginger (p.71)
Snack: Garlic Green Beans (p.51)

Wednesday

Breakfast: Sweet Potato Waffles (p.35)
Lunch: Mediterranean Lentil Salad (p.47)
Dinner: Grass-Fed Beef & Vegetable Stir-Fry (p.73)
Snack: Sweet Potato Fries (p.52)

Thursday

Breakfast: Egg Salad Avocado Toast (p.29)
Lunch: Tofu and Veggie Wrap (p.49)
Dinner: Baked Cod with Mediterranean Flavors (p.70)
Snack: Caprese-Stuffed Portobello Mushrooms (p.55)

Friday

Breakfast: Southwestern Waffle with Eggs (p.31)
Lunch: Cauliflower Rice Salad (p.48)
Dinner: King Oyster Mushroom Scallops (p.76)
Snack: Black Bean & Sweet Potato Patties (p.53)

Saturday

Breakfast: Pumpkin Spice Pancakes (p.36)
Lunch: Red Rice Mexican Bowl (p.81)
Dinner: Steamed Sea Bass with Asian Flavors (p.72)
Snack: Moroccan-Spiced Squash Soup (p.103)

Sunday

Breakfast: Mushroom & Spinach Frittata (p.33)
Lunch: Thai Red Curry with Tofu over Rice (p.59)
Dinner: Lentil and Brown Rice Pilaf (p.96)
Snack: Sweet Potato-Black Bean Tacos (p.56)

Week 2

Monday

Breakfast: Breakfast Burritos with Refried Beans and Veggies (p.38)
Lunch: Spinach and Chickpea Curry with Basmati Rice (p.88)
Dinner: Slow-Cooked Beef & Sweet Potato Stew (p.74)
Snack: Spiced Pumpkin & Split Pea Soup (p.107)

Tuesday

Breakfast: Avocado Toast with Sriracha (p.40)
Lunch: Chickpea Mayo (p.64)
Dinner: Stir-Fried Tofu and Vegetables (p.57)
Snack: Turnip and Fennel Soup (p.101)

Wednesday

Breakfast: Banana Oat Pancakes (p.34)
Lunch: Grilled Vegetable & Pesto Pasta (p.58)
Dinner: Wild Rice & Cranberry Pilaf (p.86)
Snack: Halloumi Peanut Curry (p.62)

Thursday

Breakfast: Scrambled Egg with Dill, Avocado & Sourdough (p.41)
Lunch: Buckwheat Noodle Stir-Fry (p.94)
Dinner: Tempeh "Fish" Fillets (p.77)
Snack: Warming Carrot & Tomato Soup (p.99)

Friday

Breakfast: Blueberry, Banana & Chia Muffins (p.37)
Lunch: Garlic and Chili Veggie Stir-Fry Noodles (p.61)
Dinner: Farro Risotto with Butternut Squash and Kale (p.92)
Snack: Mexican-Style Pinto Bean Soup (p.109)

Saturday

Breakfast: Smoked Salmon & Omelet (p.30)
Lunch: Teff and Vegetable Pilaf (p.80)
Dinner: Spaghetti Squash Garlic Noodles (p.90)
Snack: Chickpea Sweet Potato Stew (p.113)

Sunday

Breakfast: Chia Pudding with Flax, Hemp & Goji Berries (p.42)
Lunch: Amaranth Porridge Bowl (p.83)
Dinner: Moroccan-Spiced Squash Soup (p.103)
Snack: Garlic and Chili Veggie Stir-Fry Noodles (p.61)

Week 3

Monday

Breakfast: Egg & Veggie Burrito (p.32)
Lunch: Turmeric Chickpea Salad (p.45)
Dinner: Baked Cod with Mediterranean Flavors (p.70)
Snack: Garlic Green Beans (p.51)

Tuesday

Breakfast: Breakfast Burritos with Refried Beans and Veggies (p.38)
Lunch: Cauliflower Rice Salad (p.48)
Dinner: Steamed Sea Bass with Asian Flavors (p.72)
Snack: Moroccan-Spiced Squash Soup (p.103)

Wednesday

Breakfast: Mushroom & Spinach Frittata (p.33)
Lunch: Arugula and Beet Salad (p.46)
Dinner: King Oyster Mushroom Scallops (p.76)

Snack: Spiced Pumpkin & Split Pea Soup (p.107)

Thursday

Breakfast: Banana Oat Pancakes (p.34)
Lunch: Mediterranean Lentil Salad (p.47)
Dinner: Grass-Fed Beef and Vegetable Stir-Fry (p.73)
Snack: Chickpea Sweet Potato Stew (p.113)

Friday

Breakfast: Sweet Potato Waffles (p.35)
Lunch: Red Rice Mexican Bowl (p.81)
Dinner: Wild Rice & Cranberry Pilaf (p.86)
Snack: Warming Carrot & Tomato Soup (p.99)

Saturday

Breakfast: Pumpkin Spice Pancakes (p.36)
Lunch: Thai Red Curry with Tofu over Rice (p.59)
Dinner: Lentil and Brown Rice Pilaf (p.96)
Snack: Mexican-Style Pinto Bean Soup (p.109)

Sunday

Breakfast: Smoked Salmon & Omelet (p.30)
Lunch: Teff and Vegetable Pilaf (p.80)
Dinner: Spaghetti Squash Garlic Noodles (p.90)
Snack: Garlic and Chili Veggie Stir-Fry Noodles (p.61)

Week 4

This week follows a repeat structure, allowing you to mix and match meals based on your favorites from the previous weeks. Feel free to swap dishes, adjust portions, and explore different spice variations to keep meals exciting and enjoyable.

FOOD ELIMINATION TRACKER

DATE:

INGREDIENTS ELIMINATED	FLARE UP NOTICED

NOTES:

DATE:

INGREDIENTS ELIMINATED	FLARE UP NOTICED

NOTES:

DATE:

INGREDIENTS ELIMINATED	FLARE UP NOTICED

NOTES:

DATE:

INGREDIENTS ELIMINATED	FLARE UP NOTICED

NOTES:

DATE:

INGREDIENTS ELIMINATED	FLARE UP NOTICED

NOTES:

FOOD REINTRODUCTION DIARY

DATE:

INGREDIENTS REINTRODUCED	FLARE UP NOTICED

NOTES:

DATE:

INGREDIENTS REINTRODUCED	FLARE UP NOTICED

NOTES:

Nom Nom your Way to not Feeling like Garbage | **Irene Fields**

DATE:

INGREDIENTS REINTRODUCED	FLARE UP NOTICED

NOTES:

DATE:

INGREDIENTS REINTRODUCED	FLARE UP NOTICED

NOTES:

Nom Nom your Way to not Feeling like Garbage | **Irene Fields**

DATE:

INGREDIENTS REINTRODUCED	FLARE UP NOTICED

NOTES:

DATE:

INGREDIENTS REINTRODUCED	FLARE UP NOTICED

NOTES:

RECIPE INDEX

A
- Amaranth Porridge Bowl – p.83
- Arugula and Beet Salad – p.46
- Avocado & Kale Omelet – p.28
- Avocado Toast with Sriracha – p.40

B
- Baked Cod with Mediterranean Flavors – p.70
- Banana Oat Pancakes – p.34
- Black Bean & Sweet Potato Patties – p.53
- Black Rice Asian Bowl – p.84
- Blueberry, Banana & Chia Muffins – p.37
- Breakfast Burritos with Refried Beans and Veggies – p.38
- Buckwheat Noodle Stir-Fry – p.94
- Butternut Squash Thai Curry – p.105

C
- Caprese-Stuffed Portobello Mushrooms – p.55
- Cauliflower Rice Salad – p.48
- Chia Pudding Topped with Flax, Hemp, and Goji Berries – p.42
- Chickpea Mayo – p.64
- Chickpea Sweet Potato Stew – p.113
- Egg & Veggie Burrito – p.32
- Farro Risotto With Butternut Squash and Kale – p.92
- Garlic & Chili Veggie Stir-Fry Noodles – p.61
- Garlic Green Beans – p.51
- Grilled Mackerel with Ginger – p.71
- Grilled Vegetable & Pesto Pasta – p.58
- Grass-Fed Beef and Vegetable Stir-Fry – p.73

H
- Halloumi Peanut Curry – p.62

K
- Kale and Quinoa Salad – p.44
- King Oyster Mushroom Scallops – p.76

L

- Lentil and Brown Rice Pilaf – p.96

M
- Mediterranean Lentil Salad – p.47
- Mexican-Style Pinto Bean Soup – p.109
- Moroccan-Spiced Squash Soup – p.103
- Mung Bean & Green Vegetable Soup – p.111
- Mushroom & Spinach Frittata – p.33

P
- Plant-Based Vegetable Frittata – p.65
- Poached Salmon with Herbs – p.69
- Pumpkin Spice Pancakes – p.36

R
- Red Rice Mexican Bowl – p.81

S
- Scrambled Egg with Dill, Avocado, and Feta on Sourdough – p.41
- Smoked Salmon & Omelet – p.30
- Southwestern Waffle with Eggs – p.31
- Spaghetti Squash Garlic Noodles – p.90
- Spiced Pumpkin & Split Pea Soup – p.107
- Spinach & Egg Scramble – p.27
- Spinach and Chickpea Curry with Basmati Rice – p.88
- Stir-Fried Tofu and Vegetables – p.57
- Sweet Potato & Black Bean Tacos – p.56
- Sweet Potato Fries – p.52
- Sweet Potato Waffles – p.35

T
- Teff and Vegetable Pilaf – p.80
- Tempeh "Fish" Fillets – p.77
- Thai Red Curry with Tofu Over Rice – p.59
- Tofu and Veggie Wrap – p.49
- Turmeric Chickpea Salad – p.45
- Turnip and Fennel Soup – p.101

W
- Warming Carrot & Tomato Soup – p.99
- Wild Rice & Cranberry Pilaf – p.86

Nom Nom your Way to not Feeling like Garbage | **Irene Fields**

Printed in Great Britain
by Amazon